I0413281

Prepared in cooperation with the
New York State Department of Environmental Conservation

Groundwater Quality in the Upper Hudson River Basin, New York, 2007

Open-File Report 2009–1240

U.S. Department of the Interior
U.S. Geological Survey

Cover. Winter in the Upper Hudson River Basin

Prepared in cooperation with the
New York State Department of Environmental Conservation

Groundwater Quality in the Upper Hudson River Basin, New York, 2007

By Elizabeth A. Nystrom

Open-File Report 2009-1240

U.S. Department of the Interior
U.S. Geological Survey

U.S. Department of the Interior
KEN SALAZAR, Secretary

U.S. Geological Survey
Marcia K. McNutt, Director

U.S. Geological Survey, Reston, Virginia: 2009

For product and ordering information:
World Wide Web: http://www.usgs.gov/pubprod
Telephone: 1-888-ASK-USGS

For more information on the USGS—the Federal source for science about the Earth,
its natural and living resources, natural hazards, and the environment:
World Wide Web: http://www.usgs.gov
Telephone: 1-888-ASK-USGS

Suggested citation:
Nystrom, E.A., 2009, Groundwater quality in the Upper Hudson River Basin, New York, 2007: U.S. Geological Survey
Open-File Report 2009-1240, 37 p., available only at http://pubs.usgs.gov/of/2009/1240/.

Contents

Figures

Tables

Conversion Factors, Datum, Abbreviated Water-Quality Units, and Acronyms

Multiply	By	To obtain
Length		
centimeter (cm)	0.3937	inch (in.)
foot (ft)	0.3048	meter (m)
Area		
acre	0.004047	square kilometer (km^2)
square mile (mi^2)	2.590	square kilometer (km^2)
Volume		
liter (L)	0.2642	gallon (gal)
gallon (gal)	3.785	liter (L)
Flow rate		
gallon per minute (gal/min)	0.06309	liter per second (L/s)
inch per year (in/yr)	25.4	millimeter per year (mm/yr)
Radioactivity		
picocurie per liter (pCi/L)	0.037	becquerel per liter (Bq/L)

Temperature in degrees Celsius (°C) may be converted to degrees Fahrenheit (°F) as follows:
°F=(1.8×°C)+32

Vertical coordinate information is referenced to the North American Vertical Datum of 1988 (NAVD 88).
Horizontal coordinate information is referenced to the North American Datum of 1983 (NAD 83).
Elevation, as used in this report, refers to distance above the vertical datum.

Abbreviated units used in this report:

micrograms per liter (µg/L)
micrometer (µm)
microsiemens per centimeter at 25 degrees Celsius (µS/cm at 25 °C)
milligrams per liter (mg/L)
picocuries per liter (pCi/L)
platinum-cobalt units (Pt-Co units)

Acronyms used in this report

AMCL	Alternative maximum contaminant level
CEAT	2-Chloro-6-ethylamino-4-amino-*s*-triazine
CFU	Colony-forming units
CIAT	2-Chloro-4-isopropylamino-6-amino-*s*-triazine
cICP-MS	Collision/reaction cell inductively coupled plasma-mass spectrometry
ESA	Ethanesulfonic acid
GC-MS	Gas chromatography-mass spectrometry
GPS	Global positioning system
HPLC-MS	High-performance liquid chromatography-mass spectrometry
ICP-AES	Inductively coupled plasma-atomic emission spectrometry
ICP-MS	Inductively coupled plasma-mass spectrometry
ICP-OES	Inductively coupled plasma-optical emission spectrometry
LC-MS	Liquid chromatography-mass spectrometry
LRL	Laboratory reporting level
MCL	Maximum contaminant level
MTBE	Methyl *tert*-butyl ether
NWQL	USGS National Water Quality Laboratory
NYSDEC	New York State Department of Environmental Conservation
NYSDOH	New York State Department of Health
OA	Oxanilic acid
OGRL	USGS Organic Geochemistry Research Laboratory
OIET	2-Hydroxy-4-isopropylamino-6-ethylamino-*s*-triazine
PERC	Tetrachloroethene
PVC	Polyvinyl chloride
SA	Secondary amide
SDWS	Secondary drinking-water standards
THM	Trihalomethane
TTHMs	Total trihalomethanes
USEPA	U.S. Environmental Protection Agency
USGS	U.S. Geological Survey
VOC	Volatile organic compound

Groundwater Quality in the Upper Hudson River Basin, New York, 2007

By Elizabeth A. Nystrom

Abstract

Water samples were collected from 25 production and domestic wells in the Upper Hudson River Basin (north of the Federal Dam at Troy, N.Y.) from August through November 2007 to characterize the groundwater quality. The Upper Hudson River Basin covers 4,600 square miles in upstate New York, Vermont, and Massachusetts; the study area encompasses the 4,000 square miles that lie within New York. The basin is underlain by crystalline and sedimentary bedrock, including gneiss, shale, and slate; some sandstone and carbonate rocks are present locally. The bedrock in some areas is overlain by surficial deposits of saturated sand and gravel. Of the 25 wells sampled, 13 were finished in sand and gravel deposits, and 12 were finished in bedrock. The samples were collected and processed by standard U.S. Geological Survey procedures and were analyzed for 225 physical properties and constituents, including major ions, nutrients, trace elements, radon-222, pesticides, volatile organic compounds (VOCs), and indicator bacteria.

Water quality in the study area is generally good, but concentrations of some constituents exceeded current or proposed Federal or New York State drinking-water standards; these were: color (1 sample), pH (2 samples), sodium (5 samples), nitrate plus nitrite (2 samples), aluminum (3 samples), iron (1 sample), manganese (7 samples), radon-222 (11 samples), and bacteria (1 sample). Dissolved-oxygen concentrations in samples from wells finished in sand and gravel [median 5.4 milligrams per liter (mg/L)] were greater than those from wells finished in bedrock (median 0.4 mg/L). The pH of all samples was typically neutral or slightly basic (median 7.6); the median water temperature was 9.7°C. The ions with the highest concentrations were bicarbonate (median 123 mg/L) and calcium (median 33.9 mg/L). Groundwater in the basin is generally soft to moderately hard (less than or equal to 120 mg/L as $CaCO_3$) (median hardness 110 mg/L as $CaCO_3$). Concentrations of nitrate plus nitrite in samples from sand and gravel wells (median concentration 0.47 mg/L as nitrogen) were generally higher than those in samples from bedrock wells (median estimated 0.05 mg/L as nitrogen), and concentrations in two samples exceeded established drinking-water standards for nitrate (10 mg/L as nitrogen). The trace elements with the highest concentrations were strontium [median 217 micrograms per liter (μg/L)] and iron (median 39 μg/L). The highest radon-222 activities were in samples from bedrock wells [maximum 2,930 picocuries per liter (pCi/L)] and 44 percent of all samples exceeded a proposed U.S. Environmental Protection Agency (USEPA) drinking-water standard of 300 pCi/L. Ten pesticides and pesticide degradates were detected among 11 samples at concentrations of 1.47 μg/L or less; most were herbicides or their degradates. Six VOCs were detected among 10 samples at concentrations of 4.2 μg/L or less; these included three trihalomethanes and methyl *tert*-butyl ether, tetrachloroethene, and toluene. Most detections were in samples from sand and gravel wells and none exceeded drinking-water standards. Total coliform bacteria were detected in only one sample, and fecal coliform bacteria, including *Escherichia coli*, were not detected in any sample.

Introduction

The Federal Clean Water Act Amendments of 1977 require that states monitor and report biennially on the chemical quality of surface water and groundwater within their boundaries (U.S. Environmental Protection Agency, 1997). In 2002, the U.S. Geological Survey (USGS), in cooperation with the New York State Department of Environmental Conservation (NYSDEC), developed a program to evaluate groundwater quality throughout the major river basins in New York on a rotating basis. The work parallels the NYSDEC Rotating Intensive Basin Study program, which evaluates surface-water quality in 2 or 3 of the 14 major river basins in the State each year. The groundwater-quality program began in 2002 with a pilot study in the Mohawk River Basin (Butch and others, 2003). Sampling was completed in the Chemung River Basin in 2003 (Hetcher-Aguila, 2005); the Lake Champlain (Nystrom, 2006) and Susquehanna River Basins in 2004 (Hetcher-Aguila and Eckhardt, 2006); the St. Lawrence (Nystrom, 2007a), Delaware (Nystrom, 2007b), and Genesee River Basins (Eckhardt and others, 2007) in 2005; and the Mohawk River Basin (Nystrom, 2008) and western New York (Niagara and Allegheny River Basins, and tributaries to Lake Erie and western Lake Ontario) (Eckhardt and others, 2008) in 2006. Studies in the Upper Hudson River Basin and the Oswego, Seneca, and Oneida River Basins (the Finger Lakes area) were completed in 2007.

Purpose and Scope

This report presents the findings of the 2007 study in the Upper Hudson River Basin, in which 25 groundwater-quality samples were collected from August through November 2007. This report (1) describes the hydrogeologic setting and the methods of site selection, sample collection, and chemical analysis, and (2) discusses the analytical results for physical properties and concentrations of major ions, nutrients, trace elements and radionuclides, pesticides, volatile organic compounds (VOCs), and indicator bacteria. Information about the sampled wells and results of the analyses are presented in the appendix (tables A1 through A8).

Hydrogeologic Setting

The Upper Hudson River Basin encompasses 4,600 mi^2 in upstate New York, Vermont, and Massachusetts and is defined as the part of the Hudson River Basin that lies above the Federal Lock and Dam at Troy, N.Y. (fig. 1). This study included only the 4,000-mi^2 part of the basin that lies within New York (fig. 1). The study area contains parts of eight counties (Albany, Essex, Fulton, Hamilton, Rensselaer, Saratoga, Warren, and Washington, fig. 1). Major tributaries to the Upper Hudson River include the Schroon River, Sacandaga River, Batten Kill, and Hoosic River. The Champlain Canal, which connects the Hudson River to Lake Champlain, exits the basin north of Glens Falls. A dam on the Sacandaga River, completed in 1930, created the Great Sacandaga Lake; the dam is used for flow regulation and for power generation.

The highest elevations in the basin are more than 5,000 ft above NAVD 88 in the northern part of the basin (fig. 2). The highest elevation is at the summit of Mount Marcy, on the northern border of the basin (fig. 2). The area of greatest precipitation in the basin is in the Adirondack Park (fig. 1), where the western edge of the basin receives more than 50 in/yr (Randall, 1996). Land use (fig. 3) reflects the terrain of the basin; developed areas and agriculture are mainly in the low-lying southeastern third of the basin, although sparse urban areas are found in the northern part of the basin along the Interstate Route 87 corridor (fig. 1). The largest urban centers in the basin are the outlying parts of the Albany-Schenectady-Troy area and the cities of Glens Falls and Saratoga Springs (fig. 1). The upland areas of the basin are predominantly forested (Vogelmann and others, 2001) (fig. 3), and much of upland area lies within the Adirondack State Park. The Adirondack Park was created in 1892 and has an area of nearly 6 million acres. The New York State Constitution specifies that forest preserve in the parks "shall be forever kept as wild forest lands." About two-thirds of the basin is within the park.

Bedrock in the Upper Hudson River Basin (fig. 4) consists of mostly crystalline and sedimentary rock (Isachsen and others, 2000). The northern part of the basin is underlain by crystalline metamorphic bedrock composed mainly of gneiss; the southern part is underlain mainly by shale and slate, although some sandstones are present. Carbonate bedrock is present in a few locations throughout the basin (fig. 4). The carbonate units are generally the bedrock aquifers with the highest yields in the basin; the sandstone and shale aquifers generally produce small to moderate yields, and the crystalline metamorphic bedrock generally produces the lowest yields (Hammond and others, 1978).

The surficial material throughout the basin was deposited primarily during the Pleistocene epoch, when the Wisconsin glaciers covered most of the Northeast. Till was deposited by glaciers over most of the basin (fig. 5); sand and gravel deposits occur mainly in valleys. Till generally has low yields, whereas sand and gravel, including alluvium, outwash, and ice-contact deposits, form the most productive aquifers in the basin. Wells finished in these coarse deposits may yield as much as 1,000 gal/min (Phillips and Hanchar, 1996).

Methods of Investigation

The methods used in this study, including (1) well-selection criteria, (2) sampling methods, and (3) analytical methods, were designed to maximize data precision, accuracy, and comparability. Groundwater-sample collection and processing followed standard USGS procedures as documented in the National Field Manual for the Collection of Water-Quality Data (U.S. Geological Survey, variously dated). Samples were analyzed by documented methods at the USGS National Water Quality Laboratory (NWQL) in Denver, Colo., the USGS Organic Geochemistry Research Laboratory (OGRL) in Lawrence, Kans., and New York State Department of Health (NYSDOH)-certified laboratories.

Site Selection

Wells were selected to provide adequate spatial coverage of the basin; areas of greatest groundwater use were emphasized. The final selection was based on the availability of well-construction data and hydrogeologic information for each well and its surrounding area. The study did not target specific municipalities, industries, or agricultural practices. The 25 wells selected for sampling represented forested, rural, residential, and agricultural areas (fig. 3). The characteristics of the wells sampled and the type of land cover surrounding each well are listed in table 1. The depths of the wells, the geologic units from which samples were collected, and the numbers of production and domestic wells are summarized in table 2.

The 13 domestic wells were selected on the basis of information from the NYSDEC Water Well program, which began in 2000. The program requires that licensed well drillers file a report with NYSDEC containing basic information about each well drilled—such as well and casing depth and diameter, yield, and a hydrogeologic log. Inspection of well-completion reports identified about 200 wells as potential sampling sites. The well owners were sent a letter that included a request for permission to sample the well and a questionnaire about the well. Well owners who granted permission were contacted later by phone to verify well information and to arrange a convenient time for sampling.

Production wells considered for sampling were identified through the U.S. Environmental Protection Agency (USEPA) Safe Drinking Water Information System and the NYSDEC Water Well program. Town officials and (or) water managers were sent letters requesting permission to sample a

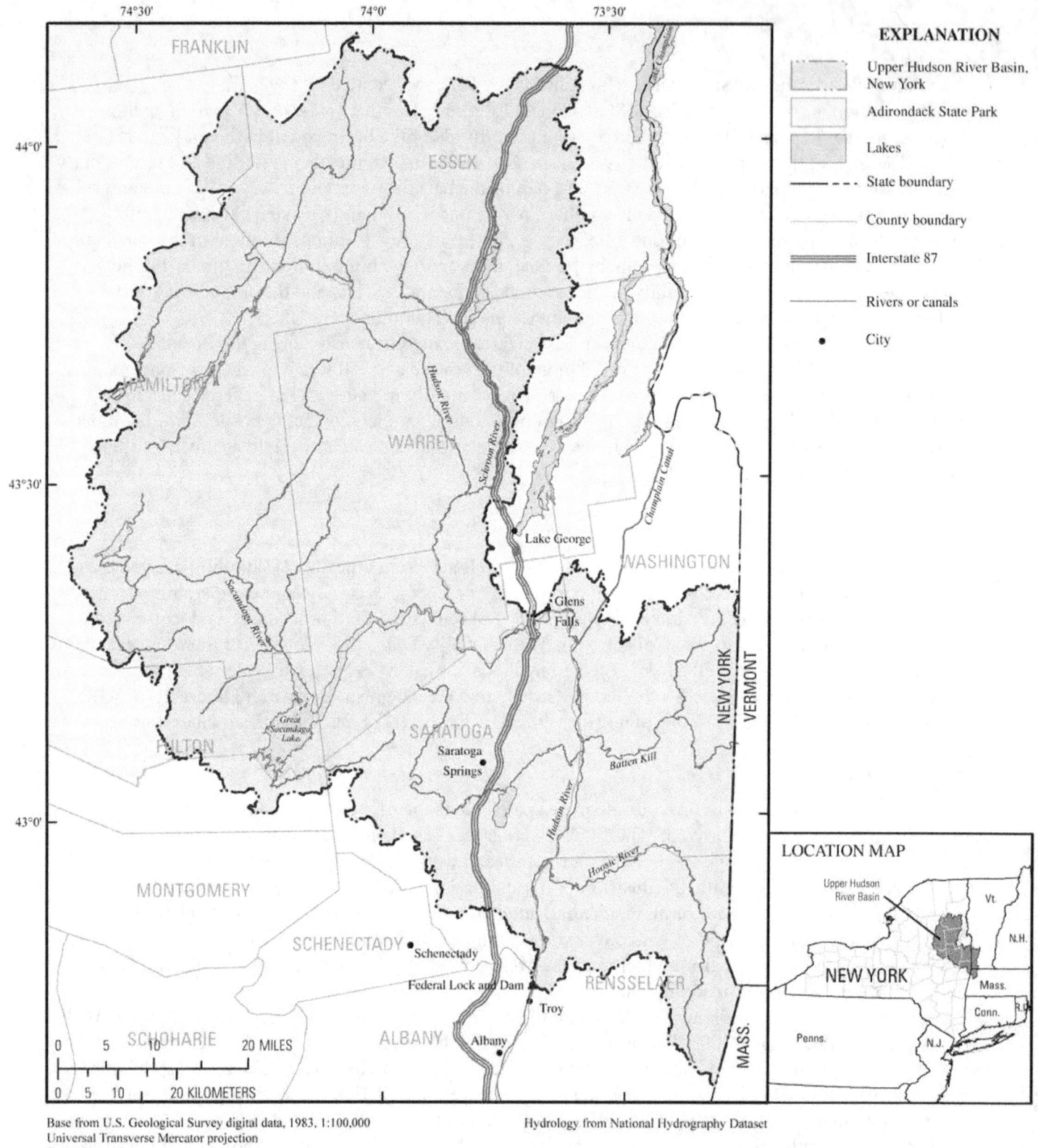

Base from U.S. Geological Survey digital data, 1983, 1:100,000
Universal Transverse Mercator projection
Zone 18

Hydrology from National Hydrography Dataset

Figure 1. Principal geographic features of the Upper Hudson River Basin in New York.

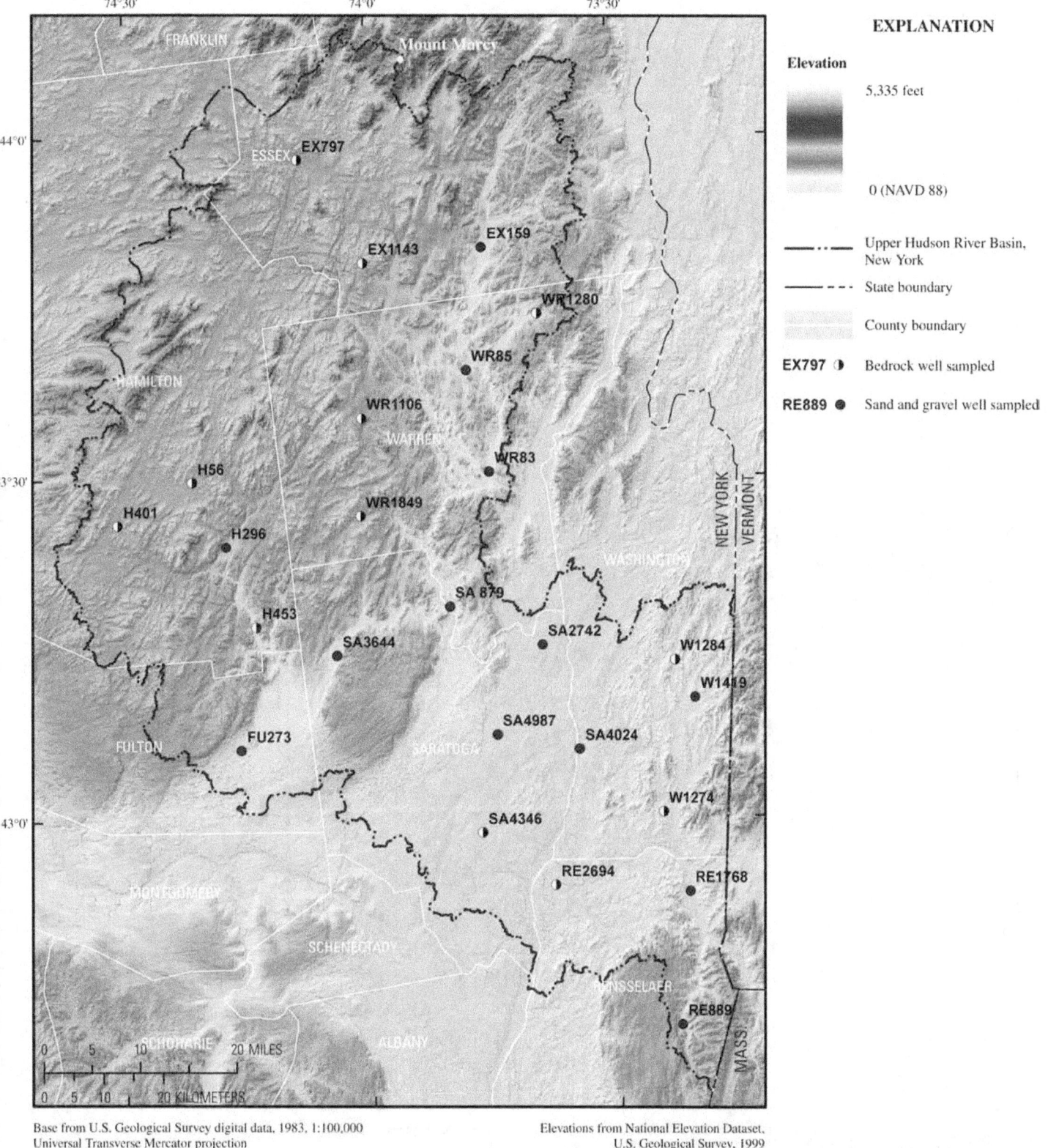

Figure 2.   Topography of the Upper Hudson River Basin in New York, and locations of wells sampled in 2007.

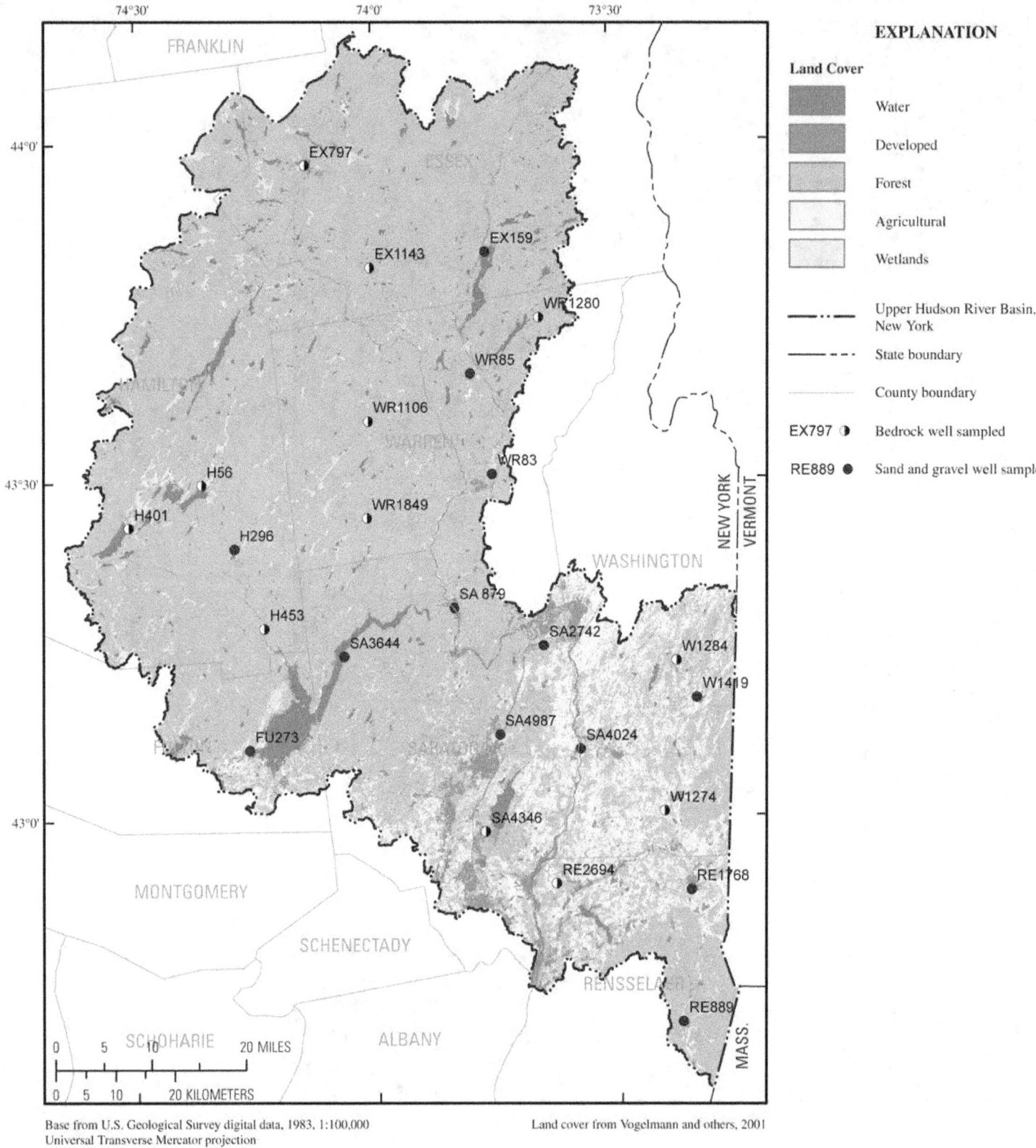

Figure 3.   Land cover of the Upper Hudson River Basin in New York, and locations of wells sampled in 2007.

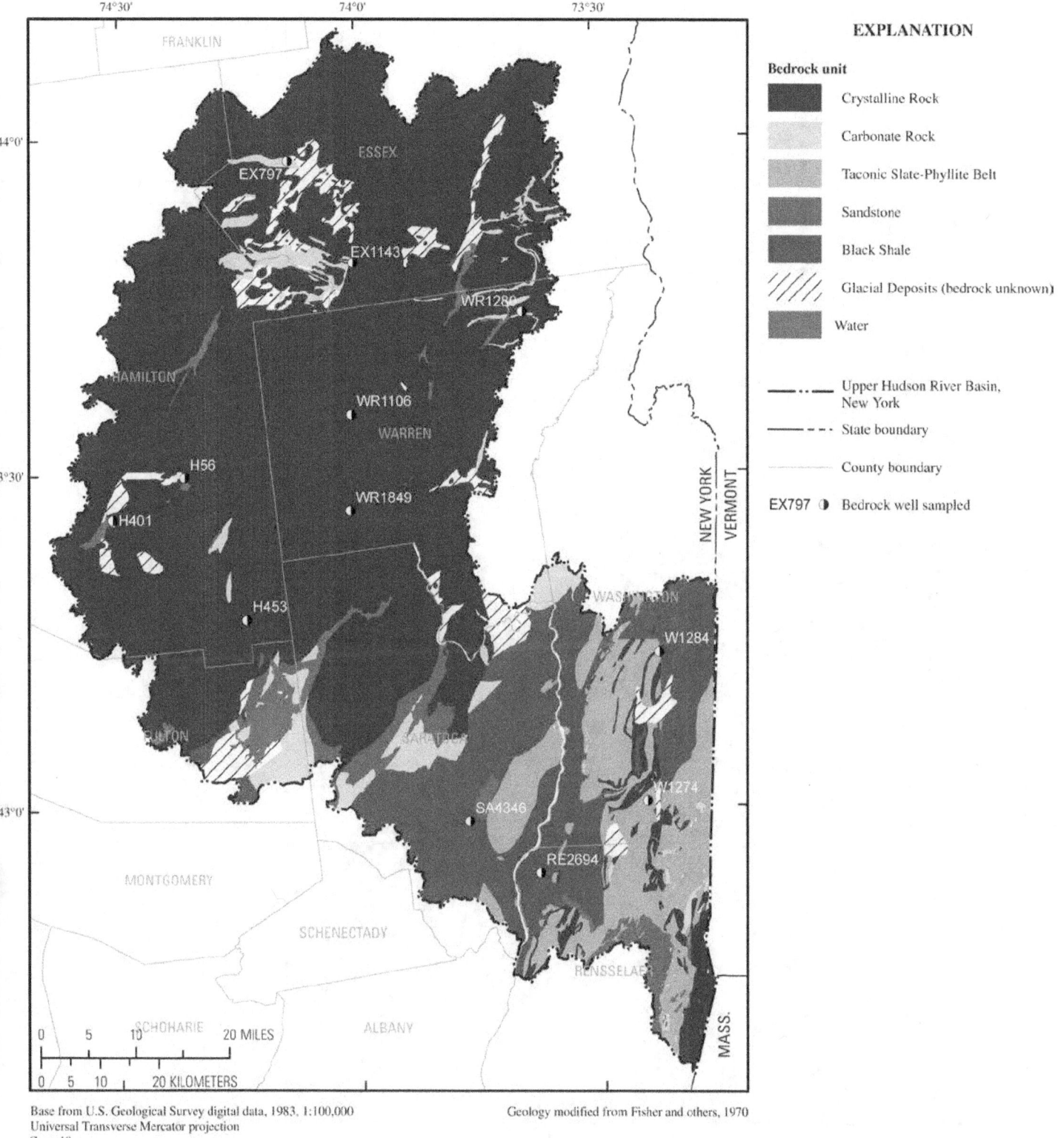

EXPLANATION

Bedrock unit

Crystalline Rock

Carbonate Rock

Taconic Slate-Phyllite Belt

Sandstone

Black Shale

Glacial Deposits (bedrock unknown)

Water

—··—··— Upper Hudson River Basin, New York

— — — State boundary

——— County boundary

EX797 ◑ Bedrock well sampled

Base from U.S. Geological Survey digital data, 1983, 1:100,000
Universal Transverse Mercator projection
Zone 18

Geology modified from Fisher and others, 1970

Figure 4. Generalized bedrock geology of the Upper Hudson River Basin in New York, and locations of wells finished in bedrock sampled in 2007.

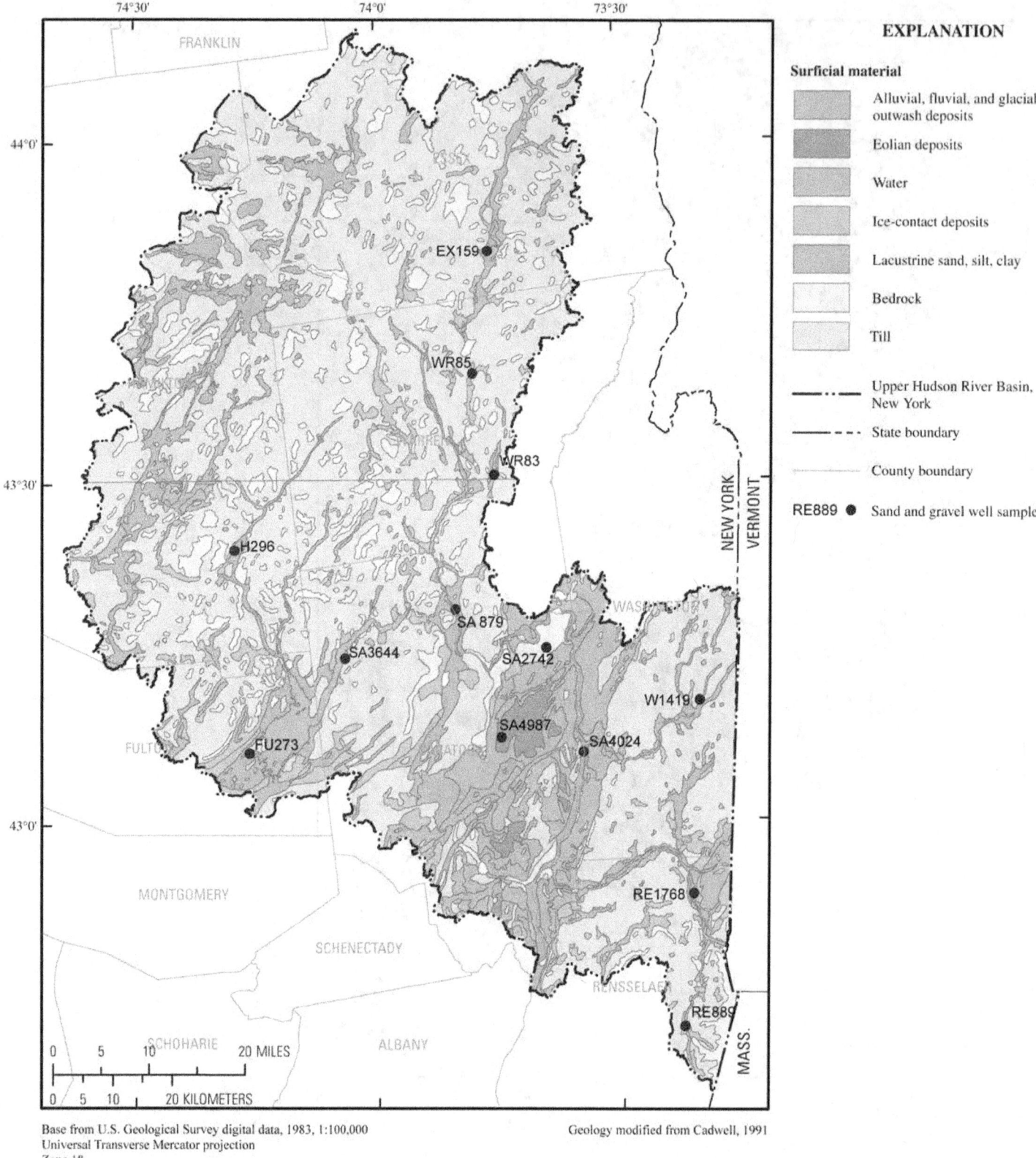

Figure 5. Generalized surficial geology of the Upper Hudson River Basin in New York, and locations of wells finished in sand and gravel deposits sampled in 2007.

well, and follow-up phone calls were made to arrange a time for sampling. Well information such as depth was provided by water managers if a well-completion report for a specific well was unavailable. The aquifer type indicated for sampled wells was verified through inspection of published geologic maps including Fisher and others (1970) and Cadwell (1991).

Table 1. Information on wells from which water samples were collected in the Upper Hudson River Basin, New York, 2007.

[--, unknown; Prod., production well; Dom., domestic well; Devel. ▓, developed; Forest ░, forested; Agric. ☐, agricultural; Water ☐, wetlands and open water. Well locations are shown in fig. 2.]

Well number[1]	Date sampled	Well depth (feet below land surface)	Casing depth (feet below land surface)	Well type	Bedrock type	Land cover[2] by category (percent) Devel.	Forest	Agric.	Water
Sand and gravel wells									
EX159	8/15/2007	196	184	Prod.	--	30	40	11	19
FU273	8/30/2007	42	--	Prod.	--		52	33	6	9
H296	10/17/2007	59	44	Prod.	--	7	58	7	28
RE889	11/1/2007	80	60	Prod.	--	25	58		17
RE1768	10/18/2007	76	61	Prod.	--		60	32	5 3
SA879	8/28/2007	87	69	Prod.	--	30	47		22
SA2742	11/6/2007	54	48	Dom.	--	4	76		20
SA3644	9/4/2007	126	126	Dom.	--		53	46	
SA4024	8/28/2007	88.5	70.5	Prod.	--	36	21	23	20
SA4987	10/18/2007	50	38	Prod.	--	18	72		10
W1419	10/16/2007	67	57	Prod.	--	21	52	25	2
WR83	8/29/2007	33	--	Prod.	--		51	28	20
WR85	11/29/2007	43	33	Prod.	--	14	75		11
Bedrock wells									
EX797	8/16/2007	120	40	Dom.	Carbonate	10	53		36
EX1143	10/15/2007	400	20	Dom.	Carbonate		100		
H56	8/27/2007	536	80	Prod.	Crystalline	26	29		43
H401	8/27/2007	160	95.5	Dom.	Crystalline	9	49		40
H453	8/30/2007	400	40.5	Dom.	Crystalline		80	13	7
RE2694	9/17/2007	200	105	Dom.	Shale	16	77		6
SA4346	11/5/2007	86	69	Dom.	Shale	61		38	
W1274	11/20/2007	140	40	Dom.	Carbonate		51	47	2
W1284	10/16/2007	160	40	Dom.	Shale	9	68		23
WR1106	10/15/2007	200	20	Dom.	Crystalline		99		1
WR1280	9/5/2007	805	38	Dom.	Crystalline		96		2
WR1849	9/4/2007	218	160	Dom.	Crystalline		76	20	4

[1] EX, Essex County; FU, Fulton County; H, Hamilton County; RE, Rensselaer County; SA, Saratoga County; W, Washington County; WR, Warren County.

[2] Land cover, as percentage of area within a 0.5-mile radius of the well, interpreted from National Land Cover Data set, 1992.

Table 2. Summary of information on wells from which water samples were collected in the Upper Hudson River Basin, New York, 2007.

[--, no wells]

Type of Well	Number of wells		
	Production	Domestic	Total
Wells finished in sand and gravel (33 to 196 feet deep)	11	2	13
Wells finished in bedrock (86 to 805 feet deep)	1	11	12
Carbonate bedrock	--	3	3
Shale bedrock	--	3	3
Crystalline bedrock	1	5	6
Total number of wells	12	13	25

Sampling Methods

The 25 wells were sampled from August through November 2007, and samples were collected and processed in accordance with documented USGS protocols (U.S. Geological Survey, variously dated). The samples were collected from a spigot between the well and the pressure tank, where possible, and before any water-treatment system, to be as representative of the aquifer water quality as possible. Most samples from domestic wells were collected from a spigot near the pressure tank; samples from production wells were collected at the spigot or faucet used for collection of raw-water samples by water managers.

One or two wells were sampled per day. Typically, samples were collected from one or more 10-ft lengths of Teflon tubing attached to a "garden-hose" type spigot located as close to the well as possible. Domestic wells were purged after the tubing was connected by running to waste for at least 20 minutes, or until at least one well-casing volume of water had passed the sampling point. Many of the production wells were pumped for at least 1 hour prior to sampling, typically at rates of about 100 gal/min. Domestic wells were purged at pumping rates ranging from about 2 to 5 gal/min. Wells that had been used recently required removal of less than three well-casing volumes. During well purging, notes about the well and surrounding land and land use were taken, and a global positioning system (GPS) measurement of latitude and longitude was made. After the well was purged, field measurements of water temperature, pH, specific conductance, and dissolved-oxygen concentration were recorded at regular intervals until these values had stabilized, after which the sample was collected (U.S. Geological Survey, variously dated).

The flow rate for sample collection was adjusted to less than 0.5 gal/min. The Teflon sampling tube was connected to a sampling chamber constructed of a polyvinyl chloride (PVC) frame and a clear plastic chamber bag. The sampling chamber was placed on a plastic-box table with a built-in drain. Before each day of sampling, the Teflon tubing and spigot-attachment equipment were cleaned in the laboratory with a dilute phosphate-free detergent solution, followed by rinses with tap water and deionized water. Equipment for filtration of pesticide samples was rinsed with methanol. A new sampling-chamber bag was used at each site. Samples were collected and preserved in the sampling chamber according to standard USGS procedures. Sample bottles for nutrient, major-ion, and some trace-element analyses were filled with water filtered through disposable (one-time use) 0.45-μm-pore-size polyether sulfone capsule filters that were preconditioned in the laboratory with 1 L of deionized water the day of sample collection. Sample bottles for pesticide analyses were filled with water filtered through baked 0.7-μm-pore-size glass fiber filters. Acid preservation was required for trace element, VOC, and some major-ion analyses. Acid preservative was added after the collection of other samples to avoid the possibility of cross contamination by the acid preservative; for example, samples preserved with nitric acid were acidified after the collection of samples for nutrient analysis. Bacterial samples were collected in accordance with NYSDEC and NYSDOH protocols, except that the tap from which each water sample was collected was not flame sterilized. Samples for radon analyses were collected through a septum chamber with a glass syringe according to standard USGS procedures. Water samples analyzed by NYSDOH-certified laboratories were collected in bottles provided by the analyzing laboratory. All samples except those for radiochemical analyses were chilled to 4°C or less after collection and shipped by overnight delivery to the designated laboratories.

Most sampling sites had easy access to a spigot; however, some production wells did not. Wells FU273, H56, H296, SA879, SA4024, and W1419 (fig. 2 and table 1) were sampled from taps or hydrants from which water-system personnel routinely collect raw-water samples. The syringe for radon-222 sample collection at these sites was inserted directly into the flowing water in the throat of the tap or hydrant to minimize sample exposure to the atmosphere.

Analytical Methods

Samples were analyzed for 225 physical properties and constituents, including inorganic constituents, nutrients, trace elements, radionuclides, pesticides and pesticide degradates, VOCs, and bacteria. Physical properties such as water temperature, pH, dissolved oxygen concentration, and specific conductance were measured at the sampling site. Inorganic constituents, nutrients, trace elements, radon-222, pesticides and pesticide degradates, and VOCs were analyzed at the USGS NWQL in Denver, Colo.; additional pesticide and pesticide degradates were analyzed at the USGS OGRL in Lawrence, Kans. Total organic carbon and phenolic compounds were analyzed at H2M Labs in Melville, N.Y., and indicator bacteria were analyzed at St. Peter's Bender Laboratory in Albany, N.Y. Both of these laboratories are certified by NYSDOH.

Anion concentrations were measured by ion-exchange chromatography, and cation concentrations were measured by inductively coupled plasma-atomic emission spectrometry (ICP-AES), as described in Fishman (1993). Nutrients were analyzed by colorimetry, as described by Fishman (1993), and Kjeldahl digestion with photometric finish, as described by Patton and Truitt (2000). Mercury concentrations were measured through cold vapor–atomic fluorescence spectrometry according to methods described by Garbarino and Damrau (2001). Arsenic, chromium, and nickel analyses used collision/reaction cell inductively coupled plasma-mass spectrometry (cICPMS) as described by Garbarino and others (2006). The remaining trace elements were analyzed by ICP-AES (Struzeski and others, 1996), inductively coupled plasma-optical emission spectrometry (ICP-OES), and inductively coupled plasma-mass spectrometry (ICP-MS) (Garbarino and Struzeski, 1998). In-bottle digestions for trace-element analyses described by Hoffman and others (1996) were followed. Radon-222 was measured through liquid-scintillation counting (ASTM International, 2006).

Samples for pesticide analyses were processed as described by Wilde and others (2004). Pesticides and pesticide-degradates were analyzed at the NWQL through gas chromatography-mass spectrometry (GC-MS) and high-performance liquid chromatography-mass spectrometry (HPLC-MS), as described by Zaugg and others (1995), Sandstrom and others (2001), and Furlong and others (2001). Acetamide parent compounds and degradation-product analyses were done by liquid chromatography-

11

mass spectrometry (LC-MS) at the USGS-OGRL according to methods described by Lee and Strahan (2003). VOSs were analyzed by GC-MS using methods described by Connor and others (1998).

Concentrations of total organic carbon were measured by method SW-846 9060 (U.S. Environmental Protection Agency, 2004), and total phenolic compounds were analyzed by USEPA method 420.2 (U.S. Environmental Protection Agency, 1983). Indicator bacteria samples were tested for total coliform, fecal coliform, and *Escherichia coli (E. coli)* through Standard Method 9222 (American Public Health Association, 2005). A heterotrophic plate count test (SM 9215 B) also was done.

In addition to the 25 groundwater samples, one blank sample and two sequential replicate samples were collected for quality assurance. Nitrogen-purged VOC/pesticide-grade blank water and inorganic-grade blank water supplied by the USGS-NWQL were used for a laboratory equipment blank before environmental-sample collection began. The water for unfiltered constituents was run through a piece of the Teflon tubing used for sampling; water for filtered-water constituents was pumped through the Teflon tubing into cleaned, preconditioned filters. Samples were acidified in the same manner as environmental well-water samples. The only constituent that exceeded laboratory reporting levels (LRLs) in the blank was sample color, which was measured at 2 platinum-cobalt units. The differences from the sequential replicate samples were less than 5 percent for all constituents detected above the LRL in the replicate samples except for color, zinc, and heterotrophic plate count, which were detected in one replicate sample at levels close to the LRL, where small differences in concentration make large relative percent-concentration differences.

Groundwater Quality

The 25 samples were analyzed for 225 constituents and physical properties. Fewer than half (156) of these were detected above the LRLs in any sample (appendix table A1). Results for the remaining 69 constituents and properties that were detected are presented in the appendix (tables A2 through A8). Some concentrations were reported as "estimated." Estimated concentrations are typically reported where the detected value is less than the established LRL, or when recovery of a compound has been shown to be highly variable (Childress and others, 1999). Concentrations of some constituents exceeded maximum contaminant levels (MCLs) or secondary drinking-water standards (SDWS) set by the USEPA (U.S. Environmental Protection Agency, 2003) or NYSDOH (New York State Department of Health, 2007). MCLs are enforceable standards for finished water at public water supplies; they are not enforceable for private homeowner wells but are presented here as a standard for evaluation of the water-quality results. SDWS are nonenforceable drinking-water standards that typically relate to esthetic concerns such as taste, odor, or staining of plumbing fixtures.

Physical Properties

The color of samples ranged from less than (<) 1 to 35 Pt-Co units; the median sample color was 5 Pt-Co units (appendix table A2). The color of one sample, 35 Pt-Co units, exceeded the NYSDOH MCL and USEPA SDWS of 15 Pt-Co units. Dissolved oxygen concentration ranged from < 0.1 to 10.3 mg/L and was generally greater in samples from sand and gravel wells (median 5.4 mg/L) than in samples from bedrock wells (median 0.4 mg/L). Sample pH was typically near neutral or slightly basic (median 7.6 in all wells) and ranged from 6.5 to 9.3; the median pH was 7.0 in samples from sand and gravel wells and 7.8 in samples from bedrock wells. The pH of two samples (8.8 and 9.3) exceeded the USEPA SDWS range for pH (6.5 to 8.5); both samples were from bedrock wells. Specific conductance ranged from 58 to 1,100 µS/cm at 25°C and tended to be higher in samples from wells finished in sand

12

and gravel (median 550 μS/cm at 25°C) than in samples from bedrock wells (median 287 μS/cm at 25°C). Water temperature ranged from 7.6 to 13.5°C; the median temperature was 9.7°C.

Major Ions

The anion with the highest concentrations was bicarbonate (table 3 and appendix table A3); the median concentration was 123 mg/L. The cation with the greatest median concentration (33.9 mg/L) was calcium. The concentration of sodium in five samples exceeded the USEPA nonregulatory drinking-water advisory taste threshold of 60 mg/L; the maximum concentration of sodium was 105 mg/L. The concentration of chloride was generally higher in samples from wells finished in sand and gravel (median 73.2 mg/L) than in bedrock (median 3.52 mg/L) (table 3). The concentration of fluoride in samples from bedrock wells (median 0.32 mg/L) was generally higher than in samples from sand and gravel wells (median < 0.12 mg/L). Concentrations of chloride, fluoride, and sulfate did not exceed established MCLs in any sample.

Table 3. Drinking-water standards and summary statistics for concentrations of major ions in groundwater samples from the Upper Hudson River Basin, New York, 2007.

[All concentrations are in milligrams per liter in filtered water; --, not applicable; <, less than]

	Constituent	Drinking-water standard	Number of samples exceeding standard	Median (all samples)	Sand and gravel aquifers (13 samples)			Bedrock aquifers (12 samples)		
					Min	Median	Max	Min	Median	Max
Cations	Calcium	--	--	33.9	6.27	44.0	105	2.52	28.0	75
	Magnesium	--	--	6.93	1.60	7.02	25.8	1.22	4.19	12.2
	Potassium	--	--	.98	.44	1.47	3.27	.49	.84	14.7
	Sodium	60[a]	5	12.4	1.77	34.3	105	1.31	5.64	87.7
Anions	Bicarbonate	--	--	123	26	118	264	61	129	261
	Chloride	250[bc]	0	14.1	1.05	73.2	215	.39	3.52	29.7
	Fluoride	2.2[b] 2.0[c]	0	.07	<.10	<.12	.07	.06	.32	1.36
	Sulfate	250[bc]	0	10.4	5.04	13.0	23.9	<.18	8.42	82.3
Hardness, mg/L as CaCO$_3$				110	22	140	360	11	92	240
Alkalinity, mg/L as CaCO$_3$				101	21	97	216	50	106	216
Residue on evaporation, mg/L				217	39	317	609	80	180	338

[a] U.S. Environmental Protection Agency Drinking Water Advisory Taste Threshold

[b] New York State Department of Health Maximum Contaminant Level

[c] U.S. Environmental Protection Agency Secondary Drinking Water Standard

Water hardness in the basin ranged from 11 to 360 mg/L as CaCO$_3$, and 15 of 25 samples were soft to moderately hard (120 mg/L as CaCO$_3$ or less; Hem, 1985); the median hardness was 110 mg/L as CaCO$_3$. Concentrations of calcium and magnesium, and therefore water hardness, were generally greater in samples from wells finished in sand and gravel than in samples from wells finished in bedrock. The three bedrock wells finished in carbonate rock produced hard water (121 to 180 mg/L as $CaCO_3$) or very hard water (more than 180 mg/L as $CaCO_3$). Alkalinity ranged from 21 to 216 mg/L as $CaCO_3$; the median was 101 mg/L of $CaCO_3$. Residue on evaporation at 180°C, a measurement of total dissolved solids, ranged from 39 to 609 mg/L and the median was 217 mg/L.

Nutrients and Organic Carbon

The concentrations of ammonia ranged from < 0.020 to 0.505 mg/L as nitrogen (N). Concentrations of nitrate plus nitrite were generally higher in samples from sand and gravel wells than in samples from bedrock wells (table 4). Concentrations of nitrate plus nitrite ranged from < 0.04 to 13.1 mg/L as N (table 4 and appendix table A4); the median concentration was 0.47 mg/L as N in samples from sand and gravel wells and 0.05 mg/L as N (estimated) in samples from bedrock wells. Nitrite was detected in fewer than-one third of the samples and had a maximum concentration of 0.064 mg/L as N. The concentration of nitrate plus nitrite exceeded the USEPA and NYSDOH MCL of 10 mg/L as N in two samples (11.1 and 13.1 mg/L as N). The concentration of nitrite did not exceed the MCL (1 mg/L as N) in any sample. Orthophosphate concentrations ranged from 0.003 (estimated) to 0.146 mg/L as phosphorus (P). Organic carbon was detected in 10 samples, and the maximum concentration was 2.8 mg/L.

Table 4. Drinking-water standards and summary statistics for concentrations of nutrients in groundwater samples from the Upper Hudson River Basin, New York, 2007.

[All concentrations in milligrams per liter in filtered water except as noted. N, nitrogen; P, phosphorus; --, not applicable; <, less than; E, estimated.]

Constituent	Drinking-water standard	Number of samples exceeding standard	Median (all samples)	Sand and gravel aquifers (13 samples)			Bedrock aquifers (12 samples)		
				Minimum	Median	Maximum	Minimum	Median	Maximum
Ammonia plus organic N, as N	--	--	< 0.14	< 0.10	< 0.14	0.21	< 0.10	< 0.14	.55
Ammonia, as N	--	--	< .020	< .020	< .020	.138	< .020	E .014	.505
Nitrite plus nitrate, as N	10[a][b]	2	.22	E .03	.47	11.1	< .04	E .05	13.1
Nitrite, as N	1[a][b]	0	< .002	< .002	< .002	.064	< .002	< .002	.005
Orthophosphate, as P	--	--	.008	E .003	.008	.018	E .004	.011	.146
Total organic carbon, unfiltered	--	--	< 1.0	< 1.0	< 1.0	1.9	< 1.0	< 1.0	2.8

[a] U.S. Environmental Protection Agency Maximum Contaminant Level.

[b] New York State Department of Health Maximum Contaminant Level.

Trace Elements and Radionuclides

The trace elements present in the highest median concentrations in the samples were strontium (median 217 μg/L), iron (median 39 μg/L in unfiltered water; 12 μg/L in filtered water), boron (median 14 μg/L), and barium (median 10.3 μg/L) (table 5 and appendix table A5). Median concentrations of aluminum and molybdenum were greater in samples from bedrock wells than in samples from sand and gravel wells (table 5). The concentration of aluminum in three samples exceeded the USEPA SDWS range of 50 to 200 µg/L. The concentration of iron in one unfiltered sample exceeded the USEPA SDWS and NYSDOH MCL for iron of 300 µg/L. The concentration of manganese in seven unfiltered and six filtered samples exceeded the USEPA SDWS of 50 µg/L; the concentration in two filtered and three unfiltered samples exceeded the NYSDOH MCL of 300 µg/L. Drinking-water standards for antimony, arsenic, barium, beryllium, cadmium, chromium, copper, lead, mercury, selenium, silver, thallium, zinc, and uranium were not exceeded; mercury and silver were not detected in any sample (appendix table A1).

Radon-222 activities in the water samples ranged from 20 (the LRL) to 2,930 pCi/L, and the median was 280 pCi/L. The highest radon activities (greater than (>) 1,000 pCi/L) were in samples from bedrock wells. Radon is currently not regulated in drinking water; however, the USEPA has proposed a two-part standard for radon in drinking water: (1) a 300 pCi/L MCL for areas that do not implement an indoor air-radon mitigation program, and (2) an alternative MCL (AMCL) of 4,000 pCi/L for areas that do (U.S. Environmental Protection Agency, 1999). Activities in 11 (44 percent) of the samples exceeded the proposed MCL; none of the samples exceeded the proposed AMCL.

Pesticides

Ten pesticides were detected in 11 samples. Most of the pesticides detected were broadleaf herbicides or their degradates; an insecticide (fipronil) and a fungicide (metalaxyl) were also detected (appendix table A6). Pesticides were detected in eight samples from sand and gravel wells and in three samples from bedrock wells. Most detections were in hundredths or thousandths of micrograms per liter; the constituents with the highest concentrations were metolachlor degradates (maximum 1.47 µg/L). The most frequently detected pesticides were alachlor ethanesulfonic acid (ESA) (six samples), metolachlor ESA (four samples), metolachlor OA (oxanilic acid) (three samples), and CIAT (2-chloro-4-isopropylamino-6-amino-s-triazine) (three samples). No pesticide concentrations exceeded established drinking-water standards. Pesticide degradates are not currently regulated.

Volatile Organic Compounds and Phenolic Compounds

VOCs were detected in samples from 10 wells—8 finished in sand and gravel and 2 finished in bedrock (appendix table A7). Six VOCs were detected—three trihalomethanes (THMs), methyl *tert*-butyl ether (MTBE), tetrachloroethene, and toluene. THMs are byproducts that form when chlorine or bromine are used as disinfectants; THMs are also used as solvents. The THMs detected were bromodichloromethane, dibromochloromethane, and trichloromethane (chloroform). Bromodichloromethane was detected in three samples and had a maximum concentration of 0.3 µg/L; dibromochloromethane was detected in one sample at a concentration of 0.2 µg/L; and trichloromethane was detected in eight samples and had a maximum concentration of 1.0 µg/L. The USEPA and NYSDOH MCL for total trihalomethanes (TTHMs) is 80 µg/L; the maximum TTHMs in the samples was 1 µg/L (trichloromethane). MTBE, a gasoline additive, was detected in three samples; the maximum concentration (4.2 µg/L) was in a sample from a bedrock well. Tetrachloroethene (PERC), a solvent sometimes used for dry cleaning, was detected in one well at a concentration of 0.3 µg/L; the USEPA and NYSDOH MCL for tetrachloroethene is 5 µg/L. Toluene, a component of gasoline, was detected in one well at a concentration of 1.1 µg/L; the NYSDOH MCL for toluene is 5 µg/L, and the USEPA MCL is 1,000 µg/L. Phenolic compounds were detected in one sample, which was from a bedrock well, at a concentration of 5.1 µg/L.

Table 5. Drinking-water standards and summary statistics for concentrations of trace elements and radionuclides in groundwater samples from the Upper Hudson River Basin, New York, 2007.

[µg/L, micrograms per liter; <, less than; E, estimated value; --, not applicable; pCi/L, picocuries per liter]

Constituent	Drinking-water standard	Number of samples exceeding standard	Median (all samples)	Sand and gravel aquifers (13 samples)			Bedrock aquifers (12 samples)		
				Minimum	Median	Maximum	Minimum	Median	Maximum
Aluminum, unfiltered, µg/L	50-200[c]	3	E 2	< 2	E 1	E 3	< 4	4	2,100
Antimony, unfiltered, µg/L	6[ab]	0	< .2	< .1	< .2	E .1	< .1	< .2	.3
Arsenic, unfiltered, µg/L	10[ab]	2	E .14	< .20	< .60	1.6	< .20	E .43	3.7
Barium, unfiltered, µg/L	2,000[ab]	0	10.3	1.4	11.1	216	1.1	5.9	507
Beryllium, unfiltered, µg/L	4[ab]	0	< .06	< .04	< .04	< .06	< .04	< .06	.09
Boron, filtered, µg/L	--	--	14	4.0	12	110	4.5	41	266
Cadmium, unfiltered, µg/L	5[ab]	0	E .01	< .01	< .02	.16	< .01	E .01	.11
Chromium, unfiltered, µg/L	100[ab]	0	< .60	< .40	< .60	1.1	< .40	< .60	2.7
Cobalt, unfiltered, µg/L	--	--	E .03	< .04	E .03	.61	< .04	.04	.59
Copper, unfiltered, µg/L	1,000[c]	0	2.1	< 1.2	2.8	50.3	< 1.2	E 1.1	13.1
Iron, filtered, µg/L	300[bc]	0	12	< 6	12	149	< 6	10	90
Iron, unfiltered, µg/L	300[bc]	1	39	< 6	35	190	< 6	78	2,110
Lead, unfiltered, µg/L	15[d]	0	.22	< .06	.16	3.77	E .05	.29	1.34
Lithium, unfiltered, µg/L	--	--	2.0	< .4	1.1	6.1	.6	3.8	148
Manganese, filtered, µg/L	50[c] 300[b]	6 2	2.4	< .4	1.1	776	< .4	2.5	342
Manganese, unfiltered, µg/L	50[c] 300[b]	7 3	3.4	< .4	1.0	780	< .4	3.6	334
Molybdenum, unfiltered, µg/L	--	--	.7	< .1	.2	1.0	.4	1.8	37.8
Nickel, unfiltered, µg/L	--	--	.21	< .12	.20	1.9	E .10	.25	55.3
Selenium, unfiltered, µg/L	50[ab]	0	< .08	< .08	E .04	.22	< .08	< .08	.54
Strontium, unfiltered, µg/L	--	--	217	22.0	198	402	34.2	288	712
Zinc, unfiltered, µg/L	5,000[bc]	0	2.4	< 2.0	2.3	214	< 2.0	3.2	32.4
Radon-222, unfiltered, pCi/L	300[e]	11	280	60	280	940	20	420	2,930
Uranium, unfiltered, µg/L	30[a]	0	.367	.021	.330	2.01	< .020	.464	3.39

[a] U.S. Environmental Protection Agency Maximum Contaminant Level.
[b] New York State Department of Health Maximum Contaminant Level.
[c] U.S. Environmental Protection Agency Secondary Drinking Water Standard.
[d] U.S. Environmental Protection Agency Treatment Technique.
[e] U.S. Environmental Protection Agency Proposed Maximum Contaminant Level.
[f] Constituent detected but not quantified.

Pesticides

Ten pesticides were detected in 11 samples. Most of the pesticides detected were broadleaf herbicides or their degradates; an insecticide (fipronil) and a fungicide (metalaxyl) were also detected (appendix table A6). Pesticides were detected in eight samples from sand and gravel wells and in three samples from bedrock wells. Most detections were in hundredths or thousandths of micrograms per liter; the constituents with the highest concentrations were metolachlor degradates (maximum 1.47 μg/L). The most frequently detected pesticides were alachlor ethanesulfonic acid (ESA) (six samples), metolachlor ESA (four samples), metolachlor OA (oxanilic acid) (three samples), and CIAT (2-chloro-4-isopropylamino-6-amino-*s*-triazine) (three samples). No pesticide concentrations exceeded established drinking-water standards. Pesticide degradates are not currently regulated.

Volatile Organic Compounds and Phenolic Compounds

VOCs were detected in samples from 10 wells—8 finished in sand and gravel and 2 finished in bedrock (appendix table A7). Six VOCs were detected—three trihalomethanes (THMs), methyl *tert*-butyl ether (MTBE), tetrachloroethene, and toluene. THMs are byproducts that form when chlorine or bromine are used as disinfectants; THMs are also used as solvents. The THMs detected were bromodichloromethane, dibromochloromethane, and trichloromethane (chloroform). Bromodichloromethane was detected in three samples and had a maximum concentration of 0.3 μg/L; dibromochloromethane was detected in one sample at a concentration of 0.2 μg/L; and trichloromethane was detected in eight samples and had a maximum concentration of 1.0 μg/L. The USEPA and NYSDOH MCL for total trihalomethanes (TTHMs) is 80 μg/L; the maximum TTHMs in the samples was 1 μg/L (trichloromethane). MTBE, a gasoline additive, was detected in three samples; the maximum concentration (4.2 μg/L) was in a sample from a bedrock well. Tetrachloroethene (PERC), a solvent sometimes used for dry cleaning, was detected in one well at a concentration of 0.3 μg/L; the USEPA and NYSDOH MCL for tetrachloroethene is 5 μg/L. Toluene, a component of gasoline, was detected in one well at a concentration of 1.1 μg/L; the NYSDOH MCL for toluene is 5 μg/L, and the USEPA MCL is 1,000 μg/L. Phenolic compounds were detected in one sample, which was from a bedrock well, at a concentration of 5.1 μg/L.

Bacteria

Total coliform bacteria were detected in one sample from a bedrock well (appendix table A8). The NYSDOH and USEPA MCL for total coliform bacteria is exceeded when 5 percent of samples of finished water collected in 1 month test positive for total coliform (if 40 or more samples are collected per month) or when two samples are positive for total coliform (if fewer than 40 samples are collected per month). The owner of the well was notified of the detection upon receipt of the results from the laboratory. Fecal coliform and *E. coli* were not detected in any sample. The heterotrophic plate count ranged from < 1 colony-forming unit (CFU) per mL to 252 CFU/mL. The USEPA MCL for the heterotrophic plate count is 500 CFU/mL; this limit was not exceeded in any sample.

Summary

Groundwater samples were collected from August through November 2007 from 13 wells finished in sand and gravel and 12 wells finished in bedrock to characterize the groundwater quality in the Upper Hudson River Basin in New York State. The wells finished in sand and gravel ranged from 33 to 196 ft deep; those finished in bedrock ranged from 86 to 805 ft deep and were typically finished in crystalline rock. Twelve of the 25 wells sampled were production wells, and 13 were domestic wells.

Sample collection and analyses followed standard USGS procedures and other documented procedures. Samples were analyzed for physical properties and for concentrations of major ions, nutrients, trace elements, radon-222, pesticides, VOCs, and bacteria. Many of the 225 constituents were not detected in any of the samples.

The samples generally indicated good water quality, although concentrations of some constituents—color, pH, sodium, nitrate, aluminum, iron, manganese, radon-222, and bacteria— exceeded primary, secondary, or proposed drinking-water standards.. The constituents most frequently detected in concentrations exceeding drinking-water standards were radon-222 (11 samples with concentrations greater than the USEPA proposed MCL of 300 pCi/L), manganese (7 unfiltered samples with concentrations greater than the USEPA SDWS of 50 µg/L), and sodium (5 samples with concentrations greater than the USEPA drinking-water advisory taste threshold of 60 mg/L). Two samples had concentrations of nitrate plus nitrite that exceeded the USEPA and NYSDOH MCL of 10 mg/L as N. No pesticide or VOC was detected above established drinking-water standards.

The water generally ranged from soft to moderately hard. Some constituents, notably dissolved oxygen and nitrate plus nitrite, were detected more frequently in samples from sand and gravel wells than in samples from bedrock wells. The highest radon-222 activities were in samples from bedrock wells (maximum 2,930 pCi/L). Ten pesticides and pesticide degradates were detected in eight samples from sand and gravel wells and in three samples from bedrock wells; most were trace-level detections of broadleaf herbicides or their degradates. Most VOC detections were in samples from sand and gravel wells; these included three trihalomethanes plus MTBE, toluene, and tetrachloroethene. No VOC concentrations exceeded drinking-water standards.

References Cited

American Public Health Association, 2005, Standard methods for the examination of water and wastewater (21st ed.): Washington, D.C., American Public Health Association, American Water Works Association, and Water Environment Federation [variously paged].

ASTM International, 2006, D5072-98(2006), Standard test method for radon in drinking water: ASTM International, accessed December 28, 2006, at *http://www.astm.org*

Butch, G.K., Murray, P.M., Hebert, G.J., and Weigel, J.F., 2003, Water Resources Data, New York, Water Year 2002: U.S. Geological Survey Water-Data Report, NY-02-1, p. 502-520.

Cadwell, D.H., 1991, Surficial geologic map of New York: New York State Museum Map and Chart Series no. 40, Adirondack sheet, scale 1:250,000.

Childress, C.J.O., Foreman, W.T., Connor, B.F., and Maloney, T.J., 1999, New reporting procedures based on long-term method detection levels and some considerations for interpretations of water-quality data provided by the U.S. Geological Survey National Water Quality Laboratory: U.S. Geological Survey Open-File Report 99-193, 19 p.

Connor, B.F., Rose, D.L., Noriega, M.C., Murtagh, L.K., and Abney, S.R., 1998, Methods of analysis by the U.S. Geological Survey National Water Quality Laboratory—Determination of 86 volatile organic compounds in water by gas chromatography/mass spectrometry, including detections less than reporting limits: U.S. Geological Survey Open-File Report 97-829, 78 p.

Eckhardt, D.A., Reddy, J.E., and Tamulonis, K.L., 2007, Ground-water quality in the Genesee River Basin, New York, 2005-06: U.S. Geological Survey Open-File Report 2007-1093, 26 p., online only at *http://pubs.usgs.gov/of/2007/1093/*.

Eckhardt, D.A., Reddy, J.E., and Tamulonis, K.L., 2008, Ground-water quality in western New York, 2006: U.S. Geological Survey Open-File Report 2008-1140, 36 p., online only at *http://pubs.usgs.gov/of/2008/1140/*.

Fisher, D.W., Isachsen, Y.W., and Rickard, L.V., 1970, Geologic map of New York State: New York State Museum Map and Chart Series no. 15, Adirondack sheet, scale 1:250,000.

Fishman, M.J., ed., 1993, Methods of analysis by the U.S. Geological Survey National Water Quality Laboratory—Determination of inorganic and organic constituents in water and fluvial sediments: U.S. Geological Survey Open-File Report 93-125, 217 p.

Furlong, E.T., Anderson, B.D., Werner, S.L., Soliven, P.P., Coffey, L.J., and Burkhardt, M.R., 2001, Methods of analysis by the U.S. Geological Survey National Water Quality Laboratory— Determination of pesticides in water by graphitized carbon-based solid-phase extraction and high-performance liquid chromatography/mass spectrometry: U.S. Geological Survey Water-Resources Investigation Report 01-4134, 73 p.

Garbarino, J.R., and Damrau, D.L., 2001, Methods of analysis by the U.S. Geological Survey National Water Quality Laboratory—Determination of organic plus inorganic mercury in filtered and unfiltered natural water with cold vapor—atomic fluorescence spectrometry: U.S. Geological Survey Water-Resources Investigation Report 01-4132, 16 p.

Garbarino, J.R., Kanagy, L.K., and Cree, M.E., 2006, Determination of elements in natural-water, biota, sediment and soil samples using collision/reaction cell inductively coupled plasma-mass spectrometry: U.S. Geological Survey Techniques and Methods, book 5, sec. B, chap.1, 88 p.

Garbarino, J.R., and Struzeski, T.M., 1998, Methods of analysis by the U.S. Geological Survey National Water Quality Laboratory—Determination of elements in whole-water digests using inductively coupled plasma-optical emission spectrometry and inductively coupled plasma-mass spectrometry: U.S. Geological Survey Open-File Report 98-165, 101 p.

Hammond, D.S., Heath, R.C., and Waller, R.M., 1978, Ground-water data on the Hudson River Basin, New York: U.S. Geological Survey Open-File Report 78-710, 18 p.

Hem, J.D., 1985, Study and interpretation of the chemical characteristics of natural water: U.S. Geological Survey Water-Supply Paper 2254, 264 p.

Hetcher-Aguila, K.K., 2005, Ground-water quality in the Chemung River Basin, New York, 2003: U.S. Geological Survey Open-File Report 2004-1329, 19 p., online only at *http://ny.water.usgs.gov/pubs/of/of041329/*.

Hetcher-Aguila, K.K., and Eckhardt, D.A., 2006, Ground-water quality in the upper Susquehanna River Basin, New York, 2004: U.S. Geological Survey Open-File Report 2006-1161, 21 p., online only at *http://pubs.usgs.gov/of/2006/1161/*.

Hoffman, G.L., Fishman, M.J., and Garbarino, J.R., 1996, Methods of analysis by the U.S. Geological Survey National Water Quality Laboratory—In-bottle acid digestion of whole-water samples: U.S. Geological Survey Open-File Report 96-225, 28 p.

Isachsen, Y.W., Landing, E., Lauber, J.M., Rickard, L.V., and Rogers, W.B., eds., 2000, Geology of New York—A simplified account (2d ed.): Albany, N.Y., New York State Museum/Geological Survey, 294 p.

Lee, E.A., and Strahan, A.P., 2003, Methods of analysis by the U.S. Geological Survey Organic Geochemistry Research Group—Determination of acetamide herbicides and their degradations products in water using online solid-phase extraction and liquid chromatography/mass spectrometry: U.S. Geological Survey Open-File Report 03-173, 17 p.

New York State Department of Health, 2007, New York State Health Department public water systems regulations: Albany, N.Y. [variously paged], accessed March 25, 2009, at *http://www.health.state.ny.us/environmental/water/drinking/part5/tables.htm*

Nystrom, E.A., 2006, Ground-water quality in the Lake Champlain Basin, New York, 2004: U.S. Geological Survey Open-File Report 2006-1088, 22 p., online only at *http://pubs.usgs.gov/of/2006/1088/*.

Nystrom, E.A., 2007a, Ground-water quality in the St. Lawrence River Basin, New York, 2005-06: U.S. Geological Survey Open-File Report 2007-1066, 33 p., online only at *http://pubs.usgs.gov/of/2007/1066/*.

Nystrom, E.A., 2007b, Ground-water quality in the Delaware River Basin, New York, 2001 & 2005-06: U.S. Geological Survey Open-File Report 2007-1098, 36 p., online only at *http://pubs.usgs.gov/of/2007/1098/*.

Nystrom, E.A., 2008, Ground-water quality in the Mohawk River Basin, New York, 2006: U.S. Geological Survey Open-File Report 2008-1086, 33 p., online only at *http://pubs.usgs.gov/of/2008/1086/*.

Patton, C.J., and Truitt, E.P., 2000, Methods of analysis by the U.S. Geological Survey National Water Quality Laboratory—Determination of ammonium plus organic nitrogen by a Kjeldahl digestion method and an automated photometric finish that includes digest cleanup by gas diffusion: U.S. Geological Survey Open-File Report 00-170, 31 p.

Phillips, P.J., and Hanchar, D.W., 1996, Water-quality assessment of the Hudson River Basin in New York and adjacent States—Analysis of available nutrient, pesticide, volatile organic compound, and suspended-sediment data, 1970-90: U.S. Geological Survey Water-Resources Investigation Report 96-4065, 77 p.

Randall, A.D., 1996, Mean annual runoff, precipitation, and evapotranspiration in the glaciated northeastern United States, 1951-80: U.S. Geological Survey Open-File Report 96-395, 2 pl., 1:250,000.

Sandstrom, M.W., Stroppel, M.E., Foreman, W.T., and Schroeder, M.P., 2001, Methods of analysis by the U.S. Geological Survey National Water Quality Laboratory—Determination of moderate-use pesticides and selected degradates in water by C-18 solid-phase extraction and gas chromatography/mass spectrometry: U.S. Geological Survey Water-Resources Investigation Report 01-4098, 70 p.

Struzeski, T.M., DeGiacomo, W.J., and Zayhowski, E.J., 1996, Methods of analysis by the U.S. Geological Survey National Water Quality Laboratory—Determination of dissolved aluminum and boron in water by inductively coupled plasma-atomic emission spectrometry: U.S. Geological Survey Open-File Report 96-149, 17 p.

U.S. Environmental Protection Agency, 1983, Methods for chemical analysis of water and wastes: Washington, D.C., U.S. Environmental Protection Agency, Environmental Monitoring and Support Laboratory Office of Research and Development, EPA 600/4-79-020, p. 420.2-1-5.

U.S. Environmental Protection Agency, 1997, Guidelines for preparation of the comprehensive state water quality assessments (305(b) Reports) and electronic updates: Washington, D.C., U.S. Environmental Protection Agency, Office of Water, EPA 841-B-97-002A and EPA 841-B-97-002B, PL95-217, 271 p.

U.S. Environmental Protection Agency, 1999, Proposed radon in drinking water rule: Washington, D.C., U.S. Environmental Protection Agency, Office of Water, EPA 815-F-99-006, 6 p.

U.S. Environmental Protection Agency, 2003, National primary drinking water standards and national secondary drinking water standards: Washington, D.C., U.S. Environmental Protection Agency, Office of Water, EPA 816-F-03-016, 6 p., available online at *http://www.epa.gov/safewater/consumer/pdf/mcl.pdf*

U.S. Environmental Protection Agency, 2004, Test methods for evaluating solid waste—Physical/chemical methods: EPA SW-846, p. 9060A1—5, available online at *http://www.epa.gov/osw/hazard/testmethods/sw846/pdfs/9060a.pdf*

U.S. Geological Survey, variously dated, National field manual for the collection of water-quality data: U.S. Geological Survey Techniques of Water-Resource Investigations, book 9, chaps. A1-A9 [variously paged].

Vogelmann, J.E., Howard, S.M., Yang, L., Larson, C.R., Wylie, B.K., and Van Driel, J.N., 2001, Completion of the 1990's National Land Cover Data Set for the conterminous United States: Photogrammetric Engineering and Remote Sensing, v. 67, p. 650-662.

Wilde, F.D., Radtke, D.B., Gibs, Jacob, and Iwatsubo, R.T., eds., April 2004, Processing of water samples (version 2.1): U.S. Geological Survey Techniques of Water-Resource Investigations, book 9, chap. A5, accessed January 11, 2007, at *http://pubs.water.usgs.gov/twri9A5/*.

Zaugg, S.D., Sandstrom, M.W., Smith, S.G., and Fehlberg, K.M., 1995, Methods of analysis by the U.S. Geological Survey National Water Quality Laboratory—Determination of pesticides in water by C-18 solid-phase extraction and capillary-column gas chromatography/mass spectrometry with selected-ion monitoring: U.S. Geological Survey Open-File Report 95-181, 60 p.

Appendix: Results of Water-Sample Analyses

The following tables summarize results of the chemical analyses of the 25 samples collected in the Upper Hudson River Basin of eastern New York from August through November 2007.

Table A1. Constituents that were not detected in groundwater samples collected in the Upper Hudson River Basin, New York, 2007.

[WY, water year, the 12-month period from October 1 through September 30 of the following year. The water year is designated by the calendar year in which it ends.]

U.S. Geological Survey parameter code	Element or compound	Laboratory reporting level	
		WY 2007	WY 2008
Trace elements in unfiltered water, micrograms per liter			
71900	Mercury	0.010	0.010
01077	Silver	.02	.02
Pesticides in filtered water, micrograms per liter			
50470	2,4-D methyl ester	.200	.200
39732	2,4-D	.04	.02
38746	2,4-DB	.02	.02
82660	2,6-Diethylaniline	.002	.002
04038	2-Chloro-6-ethylamino-4-amino-*s*-triazine (CEAT)	.08	.08
63781	2-Chloro-*N*-(2,6-diethylphenyl)acetamide	.02	.02
63782	2-Chloro-*N*-(2-ethyl-6-methylphenyl)acetamide	.02	.02
50355	2-Hydroxy-4-isopropylamino-6-ethylamino-*s*-triazine (OIET)	.080	.040
49308	3-Hydroxy carbofuran	.020	.040
61029	Acetochlor ethanesulfonic acid	.02	.02
61030	Acetochlor oxanilic acid	.02	.02
62847	Acetochlor sulfynilacetic acid	.02	.02
49260	Acetochlor	.006	.006
49315	Acifluorfen	.060	.040
62849	Alachlor ethanesulfonic acid secondary amide	.02	.02
61031	Alachlor oxanilic acid	.02	.02
62848	Alachlor sulfynilacetic acid	.02	.02
46342	Alachlor	.005	.006
49313	Aldicarb sulfone	.08	.08
49314	Aldicarb sulfoxide	.040	.060
49312	Aldicarb	.04	.12
34253	*alpha*-HCH	.002	.002
82686	Azinphos-methyl	.080	.120
50299	Bendiocarb	.04	.04
82673	Benfluralin	.006	.004
50300	Benomyl	.020	.040
61693	Bensulfuron	.06	.06
38711	Bentazon	.02	.04
04029	Bromacil	.04	.02
49311	Bromoxynil	.12	.12
04028	Butylate	.002	.002
50305	Caffeine	.040	.060
49310	Carbaryl	.02	.04
82680	Carbaryl	.060	.060
49309	Carbofuran	.060	.020
82674	Carbofuran	.020	.020

Table A1. Constituents that were not detected in groundwater samples collected in the Upper Hudson River Basin, New York, 2007.—Continued

[WY, water year, the 12-month period from October 1 through September 30 of the following year. The water year is designated by the calendar year in which it ends.]

U.S. Geological Survey parameter code	Element or compound	Laboratory reporting level	
		WY 2007	WY 2008
Pesticides in filtered water, micrograms per liter (continued)			
61188	Chloramben methyl ester	0.10	0.10
50306	Chlorimuron	.080	.080
38933	Chlorpyrifos	.005	.005
82687	cis-Permethrin	.010	.010
49305	Clopyralid	.06	.06
04041	Cyanazine	.018	.020
04031	Cycloate	.06	.02
49304	Dacthal monoacid	.02	.02
82682	DCPA	.003	.003
63778	Dechloroacetochlor	.02	.02
63777	Dechloroalachlor	.02	.02
63779	Dechlorodimethenamid	.02	.02
63780	Dechlorometolachlor	.02	.02
62170	Desulfinyl fipronil	.012	.012
39572	Diazinon	.005	.005
49302	Dichlorprop	.04	.02
39381	Dieldrin	.009	.009
61951	Dimethenamid ethanesulfonic acid	.02	.02
62482	Dimethenamid oxanilic acid	.02	.02
61588	Dimethenamid	.02	.02
49301	Dinoseb	.04	.04
04033	Diphenamid	.04	.04
82677	Disulfoton	.02	.04
49300	Diuron	.04	.04
82668	EPTC	.002	.002
82663	Ethalfluralin	.009	.009
82672	Ethoprop	.012	.012
49297	Fenuron	.04	.04
62169	Desulfinylfipronil amide	.029	.029
62167	Fipronil sulfide	.013	.013
62168	Fipronil sulfone	.024	.024
61952	Flufenacet ethanesulfonic acid	.02	.02
62483	Flufenacet oxanilic acid	.02	.02
62481	Flufenacet	.02	.02
61694	Flumetsulam	.06	.06
38811	Fluometuron	.04	.04
04095	Fonofos	.006	.010
63784	Hydroxyacetochlor	.02	.02
63783	Hydroxyalachlor	.02	.02
64045	Hydroxydimethenamid	.02	.02

Table A1. Constituents that were not detected in groundwater samples collected in the Upper Hudson River Basin, New York, 2007.—Continued

[WY, water year, the 12-month period from October 1 through September 30 of the following year. The water year is designated by the calendar year in which it ends.]

U.S. Geological Survey parameter code	Element or compound	Laboratory reporting level	
		WY 2007	WY 2008
Pesticides in filtered water, micrograms per liter (continued)			
63785	Hydroxymetolachlor	0.02	0.02
50356	Imazaquin	.04	.04
50407	Imazethapyr	.04	.04
61695	Imidacloprid	.060	.060
39341	Lindane	.004	.006
38478	Linuron	.04	.02
82666	Linuron	.060	.060
39532	Malathion	.016	.016
38482	MCPA	.06	.06
38487	MCPB	.20	.06
38501	Methiocarb	.040	.040
49296	Methomyl	.060	.120
82667	Methyl parathion	.008	.008
39415	Metolachlor	.010	.010
82630	Metribuzin	.012	.012
61697	Metsulfuron	.14	.14
82671	Molinate	.002	.002
61692	N-(4-Chlorophenyl)-N'-methylurea	.06	.12
82684	Napropamide	.018	.018
49294	Neburon	.02	.02
50364	Nicosulfuron	.10	.10
49293	Norflurazon	.04	.02
49292	Oryzalin	.04	.04
38866	Oxamyl	.04	.12
34653	p,p'-DDE	.003	.003
39542	Parathion	.010	.010
82669	Pebulate	.004	.005
82683	Pendimethalin	.020	.012
82664	Phorate	.020	.040
49291	Picloram	.12	.12
04037	Prometon	.01	.01
82676	Propyzamide	.004	.004
62766	Propachlor ethanesulfonic acid	.05	.05
62767	Propachlor oxanilic acid	.02	.02
04024	Propachlor	.010	.006
82679	Propanil	.011	.006
82685	Propargite	.02	.04
49236	Propham	.060	.040
50471	Propiconazole	.06	.04
38538	Propoxur	.040	.040

Table A1. Constituents that were not detected in groundwater samples collected in the Upper Hudson River Basin, New York, 2007.—Continued

[WY, water year, the 12-month period from October 1 through September 30 of the following year. The water year is designated by the calendar year in which it ends.]

U.S. Geological Survey parameter code	Element or compound	Laboratory reporting level	
		WY 2007	WY 2008
Pesticides in filtered water, micrograms per liter (continued)			
38548	Siduron	0.04	0.02
50337	Sulfometuron	.060	.060
82670	Tebuthiuron	.02	.02
82665	Terbacil	.040	.018
04032	Terbacil	.040	.040
82675	Terbufos	.01	.02
82681	Thiobencarb	.010	.010
82678	Triallate	.006	.006
49235	Triclopyr	.04	.08
82661	Trifluralin	.006	.006
Volatile organic compounds in unfiltered water, micrograms per liter			
34506	1,1,1-Trichloroethane	.1	.1
77652	1,1,2-Trichloro-1,2,2-trifluoroethane	.1	.1
34496	1,1-Dichloroethane	.1	.1
34501	1,1-Dichloroethene	.1	.1
34536	1,2-Dichlorobenzene	.1	.1
32103	1,2-Dichloroethane	.2	.2
34541	1,2-Dichloropropane	.1	.1
34566	1,3-Dichlorobenzene	.1	.1
34571	1,4-Dichlorobenzene	.1	.1
34030	Benzene	.1	.1
34301	Chlorobenzene	.1	.1
77093	cis-1,2-Dichloroethene	.1	.1
34668	Dichlorodifluoromethane	.2	.2
34423	Dichloromethane	.2	.2
81576	Diethyl ether	.2	.2
81577	Diisopropyl ether	.2	.2
34371	Ethylbenzene	.1	.1
50005	Methyl tert-pentyl ether	.2	.2
85795	m-Xylene plus p-xylene	.2	.2
77135	o-Xylene	.1	.1
77128	Styrene	.1	.1
50004	tert-Butyl ethyl ether	.1	.1
32102	Tetrachloromethane	.2	.2
34546	trans-1,2-Dichloroethene	.1	.1
32104	Tribromomethane	.2	.2
39180	Trichloroethene	.1	.1
34488	Trichlorofluoromethane	.2	.2
39175	Vinyl chloride	.2	.2

Table A2. Physical properties of groundwater samples collected in the Upper Hudson River Basin, New York, 2007.

[mg/L, milligrams per liter; μS/cm, microsiemens per centimeter at 25 degrees Celsius; (00080), U.S. Geological Survey National Water Information System parameter code; <, less than. Bold values exceed one or more drinking-water standards. Well locations are shown in fig. 2.]

Well number[1]	Color, platinum-cobalt units (00080)	Dissolved oxygen, mg/L (00300)	pH, field, standard units (00400)	Specific conductance, field μS/cm (00095)	Water temperature, degrees Celsius (00010)
Sand and gravel wells					
EX159	5	5.1	7.0	222	8.9
FU273	< 1	6.5	6.9	926	10.5
H296	5	8.9	7.5	186	7.6
RE889	5	3.9	6.8	643	10.9
RE1768	8	.2	7.3	633	9.9
SA879	2	6.5	6.5	58	10.4
SA2742	5	8.5	7.9	550	10.9
SA3644	5	8.9	7.8	730	9.5
SA4024	2	2.5	6.8	1,100	10.9
SA4987	2	.5	7.9	370	8.7
W1419	5	< .1	7.6	339	9.2
WR83	2	5.9	[2]7.0	319	9.8
WR85	5	5.4	6.8	806	9.7
Bedrock wells					
EX797	2	.1	7.3	362	8.6
EX1143	5	7.5	7.6	333	8.3
H56	5	10.3	7.9	241	8.1
H401	8	.6	7.6	201	9.0
H453	2	4.2	6.8	150	11.5
RE2694	**35**	.2	**9.3**	395	13.5
SA4346	5	.2	**8.8**	374	11.0
W1274	5	6.1	6.9	584	10.4
W1284	2	.3	7.8	402	10.5
WR1106	2	5.0	8.3	129	9.1
WR1280	15	.2	8.0	222	8.9
WR1849	5	.3	8.4	103	9.5

[1] EX, Essex County; FU, Fulton County; H, Hamilton County; RE, Rensselaer County; SA, Saratoga County; W, Washington County; WR, Warren County.

[2] Laboratory value.

Table A3. Concentrations of major ions in groundwater samples collected in the Upper Hudson River Basin, New York, 2007.

[mg/L, milligrams per liter; CaCO$_3$; calcium carbonate; (00900), U.S. Geological Survey National Water Information System parameter code; <, less than; E, estimated value. Bold values exceed one or more drinking-water standards. Well locations are shown in fig. 2.]

Well number[1]	Hardness, mg/L as CaCO$_3$ (00900)	Calcium, filtered, mg/L (00915)	Magnesium, filtered, mg/L (00925)	Potassium, filtered, mg/L (00935)	Sodium, filtered, mg/L (00930)	Acid neutralizing capacity, unfiltered, mg/L as CaCO$_3$ (90410)	Alkalinity, filtered, fixed end point, lab, mg/L as CaCO$_3$ (29801)
Sand and gravel wells							
EX159	110	32.1	6.19	0.68	8.84	57	57
FU273	360	105	22.7	2.02	50.1	187	213
H296	83	30.5	1.65	.44	3.15	83	83
RE889	160	49.7	8.07	2.42	**63.6**	123	122
RE1768	220	68.0	12.8	1.85	38.4	216	216
SA879	22	6.27	1.60	.50	1.77	21	21
SA2742	120	36.1	8.43	1.05	53.5	72	73
SA3644	290	74.5	25.8	1.93	12.4	49	49
SA4024	290	83.2	19.0	3.27	**105**	203	196
SA4987	120	38.5	6.93	.70	19.4	101	101
W1419	160	53.1	6.09	1.50	5.40	143	142
WR83	110	30.8	6.95	1.01	34.3	67	67
WR85	140	44.0	7.02	1.47	**93.7**	97	97
Bedrock wells							
EX797	180	53.7	10.4	.96	2.63	101	101
EX1143	170	61.1	4.63	.82	1.82	153	152
H56	100	29.7	7.28	.85	5.15	83	83
H401	88	26.4	5.46	.68	3.45	74	73
H453	63	20.1	3.10	.49	3.92	50	50
RE2694	36	8.32	3.75	1.67	**80.1**	207	214
SA4346	11	2.52	1.22	.98	**87.7**	202	202
W1274	240	75.0	12.2	14.7	17.3	164	164
W1284	110	30.5	9.19	2.24	37.6	162	162
WR1106	62	19.9	3.09	.80	1.31	59	59
WR1280	97	33.9	3.01	.52	8.49	111	111
WR1849	40	12.5	2.17	.74	6.12	51	50

[1] EX, Essex County; FU, Fulton County; H, Hamilton County; RE, Rensselaer County; SA, Saratoga County; W, Washington County; WR, Warren County.

Table A3. Concentrations of major ions in groundwater samples collected in the Upper Hudson River Basin, New York, 2007. —Continued

[mg/L, milligrams per liter; $CaCO_3$; calcium carbonate; (00900), U.S. Geological Survey National Water Information System parameter code; <, less than; E, estimated value. Bold values exceed one or more drinking-water standards. Well locations are shown in fig. 2.]

Well number[1]	Bicarbonate[2], filtered, fixed end point, lab, mg/L (29805)	Chloride, filtered, mg/L (00940)	Fluoride, filtered, mg/L (00950)	Silica, filtered, mg/L (00955)	Sulfate, filtered, mg/L (00945)	Residue on evaporation, filtered, mg/L (70300)
Sand and gravel wells						
EX159	70	42.4	<0.10	13.3	10.8	190
FU273	260	104	<.10	11.5	21.5	482
H296	101	4.50	<.12	7.00	5.04	110
RE889	149	107	E .07	7.63	13.0	347
RE1768	264	61.4	E .07	7.82	19.7	353
SA879	26	1.05	E .05	14.9	5.75	39
SA2742	89	79.1	<.12	16.9	18.5	317
SA3644	60	178	<.10	18.4	10.3	504
SA4024	239	215	E .05	13.4	21.6	609
SA4987	123	36.8	E .06	8.54	21.1	199
W1419	173	7.96	<.12	7.11	23.9	200
WR83	82	73.2	E .07	9.13	9.54	217
WR85	118	175	<.12	13.3	9.74	424
Bedrock wells						
EX797	123	.60	.14	14.4	82.3	240
EX1143	185	4.61	.17	13.0	18.2	204
H56	101	16.6	.47	15.3	10.4	157
H401	89	13.4	.12	23.3	5.69	134
H453	61	6.39	.34	12.7	9.86	102
RE2694	261	.43	.43	9.66	1.83	228
SA4346	246	2.44	1.31	7.00	<.18	223
W1274	200	29.7	E .06	10.5	36.8	338
W1284	198	14.1	.45	9.05	28.0	230
WR1106	72	.53	.25	17.2	6.99	82
WR1280	135	.64	1.36	19.3	3.31	148
WR1849	61	.39	.31	14.1	3.11	80

[1] EX, Essex County; FU, Fulton County; H, Hamilton County; RE, Rensselaer County; SA, Saratoga County; W, Washington County; WR, Warren County.
[2] Bicarbonate concentration calculated from alkalinity.

Table A4. Concentrations of nutrients and organic carbon in groundwater samples collected in the Upper Hudson River Basin, New York, 2007.

[N, nitrogen; P, phosphorus; mg/L, milligrams per liter; (00623), U.S. Geological Survey National Water Information System parameter code; <, less than; E, estimated value. Bold values exceed one or more drinking-water standard. Well locations are shown in fig. 2.]

Well number[1]	Ammonia plus organic-N, filtered, mg/L as N (00623)	Ammonia, filtered, mg/L as N (00608)	Nitrate plus nitrite, filtered, mg/L as N (00631)	Nitrite, filtered, mg/L as N (00613)	Ortho-phosphate, filtered, mg/L as P (00671)	Organic carbon, unfiltered, mg/L (00680)
Sand and gravel wells						
EX159	E 0.05	<0.020	0.21	<0.002	0.010	<1.0
FU273	E .06	<.020	2.25	<.002	.008	1.9
H296	<.14	<.020	.40	<.002	E .006	<1.0
RE889	<.14	<.020	2.65	<.002	.006	<1.0
RE1768	E .07	.043	.06	.003	.010	1.1
SA879	<.10	<.020	.09	<.002	.008	<1.0
SA2742	<.14	E .012	**11.1**	<.002	.006	<1.0
SA3644	<.10	<.020	.47	<.002	.018	<1.0
SA4024	.21	.138	.58	.003	.007	1.9
SA4987	<.14	E .014	.22	.064	.006	1.0
W1419	<.14	E .011	E .03	.010	E .003	<1.0
WR83	<.10	<.020	1.34	<.002	.012	1.3
WR85	E .07	<.020	.95	<.002	.016	<1.0
Bedrock wells						
EX797	<.10	E .020	<.06	<.002	.015	1.3
EX1143	<.14	<.020	1.25	<.002	E .004	1.1
H56	<.10	E .014	.80	.002	.016	<1.0
H401	E .10	.095	<.06	.002	.146	1.3
H453	<.10	<.020	.68	<.002	E .005	<1.0
RE2694	.55	.505	<.06	<.002	.024	<1.0
SA4346	.39	.355	<.04	<.002	.046	<1.0
W1274	E .10	<.020	**13.1**	<.002	E .004	1.8
W1284	<.14	.067	<.04	<.002	.007	<1.0
WR1106	<.14	<.020	.08	<.002	.007	<1.0
WR1280	<.10	<.020	<.06	E .001	.007	2.8
WR1849	<.10	<.020	E .05	.005	.045	<1.0

[1] EX, Essex County; FU, Fulton County; H, Hamilton County; RE, Rensselaer County; SA, Saratoga County; W, Washington County; WR, Warren County.

31

Table A5. Concentrations of trace elements and radionuclide activities in groundwater samples collected in the Upper Hudson River Basin, New York, 2007.

[µg/L, micrograms per liter; (01105), U.S. Geological Survey National Water Information System parameter code; <, less than; E, estimated value; M, presence verified but not quantified. Bold values exceed one or more drinking-water standards. Well locations are shown in fig. 2.]

Well number[1]	Aluminum, unfiltered, µg/L (01105)	Antimony, unfiltered, µg/L (01097)	Arsenic, unfiltered, µg/L (01002)	Barium, unfiltered, µg/L (01007)	Beryllium, unfiltered, µg/L (01012)	Boron, filtered, µg/L (01020)	Cadmium, unfiltered, µg/L (01027)	Chromium, unfiltered, µg/L (01034)
Sand and gravel wells								
EX159	E 2	< 0.2	0.44	2.8	< 0.06	7.5	< 0.02	< 0.60
FU273	< 2	< .2	E .14	38.6	< .06	24	< .02	E .55
H296	E 3	< .1	< .60	7.3	< .04	5.2	< .01	E .34
RE889	< 4	< .1	< .60	25.2	< .04	28	< .01	E .27
RE1768	< 4	E .1	1.3	216	< .04	14	.02	< .40
SA879	E 1	< .2	< .20	1.4	< .06	4.0	< .02	E .31
SA2742	E 2	< .1	< .60	11.1	< .04	110	.02	.54
SA3644	2	< .2	< .20	5.1	< .06	4.6	< .02	1.1
SA4024	< 2	< .2	< .20	37.6	< .06	22	.16	< .60
SA4987	< 4	< .1	1.6	27.7	< .04	14	.02	< .40
W1419	< 4	< .1	.75	148	< .04	9.0	E .01	< .40
WR83	2	< .2	< .20	10.3	< .06	7.3	.02	< .60
WR85	E 2	< .1	< .60	5.7	< .04	12	< .01	< .40
Bedrock wells								
EX797	4	< .2	E .20	16.0	< .06	66	.02	< .60
EX1143	< 4	E .1	E .49	3.7	< .04	49	.03	< .40
H56	44	< .2	< .20	3.2	< .06	11	< .02	1.1
H401	5	< .2	.57	6.6	< .06	6.8	< .02	< .60
H453	**120**	< .2	< .20	1.4	< .06	4.5	E .01	< .60
RE2694	**2,100**	E .2	.85	507	.09	266	E .01	2.7
SA4346	**63**	< .1	< .60	113	< .04	248	.06	.60
W1274	6	.3	E .56	146	< .04	33	.11	< .40
W1284	< 4	E .1	3.7	135	< .04	148	.02	< .40
WR1106	< 4	< .1	E .37	1.7	< .04	8.6	< .01	.62
WR1280	4	< .2	2.4	5.2	< .06	64	< .02	< .60
WR1849	3	< .2	E .13	1.1	< .06	11	< .02	E .52

[1] EX, Essex County; FU, Fulton County; H, Hamilton County; RE, Rensselaer County; SA, Saratoga County; W, Washington County; WR, Warren County.

Table A5. Concentrations of trace elements and radionuclide activities in groundwater samples collected in the Upper Hudson River Basin, New York, 2007. —Continued

[μg/L, micrograms per liter; (01037), U.S. Geological Survey National Water Information System parameter code; <, less than; E, estimated value; M, presence verified but not quantified. Bold values exceed one or more drinking-water standard. Well locations are shown in fig. 2.]

Well number[1]	Cobalt, unfiltered, μg/L (01037)	Copper, unfiltered, μg/L (01042)	Iron, filtered, μg/L (01046)	Iron, unfiltered, μg/L (01045)	Lead, unfiltered, μg/L (01051)	Lithium, unfiltered, μg/L (01132)	Manganese, filtered, μg/L (01056)	Manganese, unfiltered, μg/L (01055)
Sand and gravel wells								
EX159	<0.04	<1.2	<6	<6	0.23	1.0	1.1	1.0
FU273	.05	3.0	<6	<6	.19	1.1	.7	.7
H296	<.04	12.4	<8	<6	E .05	<.4	<.4	<.4
RE889	.12	<1.2	<8	<6	.22	2.0	<.4	<.8
RE1768	.09	<1.2	149	150	.12	2.9	**285**	**306**
SA879	<.04	12.5	<6	E 4	.16	E .5	.4	<.6
SA2742	.13	2.8	16	190	.09	1.3	2.8	4.0
SA3644	<.04	3.9	12	80	E .06	.7	4.7	5.1
SA4024	.61	2.1	43	42	.40	6.1	**776**	**780**
SA4987	<.04	<1.2	28	35	1.41	3.1	22.2	22.4
W1419	.11	<1.2	98	142	E .04	3.7	**90.2**	**96.8**
WR83	E .03	50.3	31	39	3.77	<.6	.5	E .3
WR85	E .02	6.5	E 5	E 5	<.06	.5	E .4	<.8
Bedrock wells								
EX797	.10	<1.2	16	51	.17	3.2	**82.2**	**88.1**
EX1143	E .02	9.8	<8	<6	.32	4.5	E .4	.5
H56	.04	4.9	<6	<6	1.32	3.1	E .1	<.6
H401	E .02	<1.2	43	201	.24	1.2	**342**	**334**
H453	.04	12.0	<6	110	.36	1.0	.5	2.1
RE2694	.59	E 1.1	14	**2,110**	.71	148	17.7	**52.3**
SA4346	E .03	<1.2	14	106	.14	58.8	2.4	3.4
W1274	.06	13.1	E 6	11	.56	16.3	.6	1.0
W1284	.25	<1.2	<8	32	1.34	62.7	**111**	**115**
WR1106	<.04	5.6	<8	<6	.12	1.1	<.4	<.4
WR1280	E .02	<1.2	90	116	E .05	8.2	14.2	18.4
WR1849	<.04	<1.2	56	185	.26	.6	2.6	3.8

[1] EX, Essex County; FU, Fulton County; H, Hamilton County; RE, Rensselaer County; SA, Saratoga County; W, Washington County; WR, Warren County.

Table A5. Concentrations of trace elements and radionuclide activities in groundwater samples collected in the Upper Hudson River Basin, New York, 2007. —Continued

[µg/L, micrograms per liter; (01062), U.S. Geological Survey National Water Information System parameter code; <, less than; E, estimated value; M, presence verified but not quantified. Bold values exceed one or more drinking-water standard. Well locations are shown in fig. 2.]

Well number[1]	Molybdenum, unfiltered, µg/L (01062)	Nickel, unfiltered, µg/L (01067)	Selenium, unfiltered, µg/L (01147)	Strontium, unfiltered, µg/L (01082)	Thallium, unfiltered, µg/L (01059)	Zinc, unfiltered, µg/L (01092)	Radon-222, unfiltered, picoCuries per liter (82303)	Uranium, unfiltered, µg/L (28011)
Sand and gravel wells								
EX159	0.7	< 0.16	E 0.06	77.1	< 0.18	< 2.0	100	0.224
FU273	E .1	.55	.22	402	< .18	4.2	**330**	.380
H296	M	< .12	< .08	229	< .08	2.1	290	.058
RE889	E .1	.16	.13	182	< .08	2.3	**940**	.197
RE1768	.8	.30	.17	248	< .08	E 1.4	200	.771
SA879	.1	.21	< .08	22.0	< .18	5.6	280	.021
SA2742	.2	.32	< .08	198	E .04	E 1.3	180	.257
SA3644	< .1	E .09	< .08	178	< .18	2.4	**330**	.368
SA4024	.4	1.9	< .08	386	< .18	7.4	**480**	.330
SA4987	.2	E .08	E .04	142	< .08	214	60	.147
W1419	1.0	.18	.14	217	< .08	E 1.8	130	.448
WR83	.2	.52	E .05	90.3	< .18	25.4	**520**	2.01
WR85	.1	.20	< .08	247	< .08	< 2.0	280	.367
Bedrock wells								
EX797	2.0	.16	< .08	377	< .18	2.0	120	.372
EX1143	1.5	.60	.15	406	< .08	5.4	70	.137
H56	1.1	.19	E .06	157	< .18	3.9	**720**	1.56
H401	.7	E .15	< .08	90.2	< .18	< 2.0	**1,550**	3.39
H453	1.1	.28	.13	47.3	< .18	10.2	**1,080**	.282
RE2694	4.6	1.8	< .08	426	< .18	3.2	20	.164
SA4346	37.8	.22	< .08	234	< .08	< 2.0	70	< .020
W1274	.4	.80	.54	471	< .08	8.3	**1,010**	1.27
W1284	8.3	1.0	< .08	712	< .08	< 2.0	120	1.22
WR1106	1.2	E .10	< .08	83.2	< .08	3.1	110	.227
WR1280	2.4	E .14	< .08	341	< .18	32.4	**1,340**	1.88
WR1849	2.2	55.3	< .08	34.2	< .18	< 2.0	**2,930**	.555

[1] EX, Essex County; FU, Fulton County; H, Hamilton County; RE, Rensselaer County; SA, Saratoga County; W, Washington County; WR, Warren County.

34

Table A6. Concentrations of pesticides detected in groundwater samples collected in the Upper Hudson River Basin, New York, 2007.

[µg/L, micrograms per liter; ESA, ethanesulfonic acid; SA, secondary amide; CIAT, 2-chloro-4-isopropylamino-6-amino-*s*-triazine; OA, oxanilic acid; (62850), U.S. Geological Survey National Water Information System parameter code; <, less than; E, estimated value; M, presence verified but not quantified. Bold values indicate detections. Well locations are shown in fig. 2.]

Well number[1]	Acetochlor/ Metolachlor ESA SA, filtered, µg/L (62850)	CIAT, filtered, µg/L (04040)	Alachlor ESA, filtered, µg/L (50009)	Atrazine, filtered, µg/L (39632)	Dicamba, filtered, µg/L (38442)	Fipronil, filtered, µg/L (62166)	Metalaxyl, filtered, µg/L (50359)	Metolachlor ESA, filtered, µg/L (61043)	Metolachlor OA, filtered, µg/L (61044)	Simazine, filtered, µg/L (04035)
Sand and gravel wells										
EX159	< 0.02	< 0.014	< 0.02	< 0.007	< 0.08	< 0.016	< 0.04	< 0.02	< 0.02	< 0.006
FU273	< .02	< .014	< .02	< .007	< .08	< .016	< .04	**.08**	< .02	< .006
H296	< .02	< .014	**.02**	< .007	< .04	< .020	< .02	< .02	< .02	< .006
RE889	< .02	< .014	**.02**	< .007	< .04	< .020	< .02	< .02	< .02	< .006
RE1768	< .02	**E .002**	**.03**	**E .002**	< .04	< .020	< .02	< .02	< .02	< .006
SA879	< .02	< .014	< .02	< .007	< .08	< .016	< .04	< .02	< .02	< .006
SA2742	< .02	< .014	< .02	< .007	< .04	**E .004**	< .02	< .02	< .02	< .006
SA3644	< .02	< .014	< .02	< .007	**.26**	< .016	< .04	< .02	< .02	< .006
SA4024	< .02	< .014	**.03**	< .007	< .08	< .016	< .04	**.05**	**.02**	< .006
SA4987	< .02	< .014	< .02	< .007	< .04	< .020	< .02	< .02	< .02	< .006
W1419	< .02	< .014	< .02	< .007	< .04	< .020	< .02	< .02	< .02	< .006
WR83	< .02	< .014	< .02	< .007	< .08	< .016	< .04	< .02	< .02	< .006
WR85	< .02	**E .002**	< .02	**E .006**	< .04	< .020	< .02	< .02	< .02	**E .005**
Bedrock wells										
EX797	< .02	< .014	< .02	< .007	< .08	< .016	< .04	< .02	< .02	< .006
EX1143	< .02	< .014	< .02	< .007	< .04	< .020	< .02	< .02	< .02	< .006
H56	< .02	< .014	< .02	< .007	< .08	< .016	< .04	< .02	< .02	< .006
H401	< .02	< .014	< .02	< .007	< .08	< .016	< .04	< .02	< .02	< .006
H453	< .02	< .014	< .02	< .007	< .08	< .016	< .04	< .02	< .02	< .006
RE2694	< .02	< .014	< .02	< .007	< .08	< .016	< .04	< .02	< .02	< .006
SA4346	< .02	< .014	< .02	< .007	< .04	< .020	< .02	< .02	< .02	< .006
W1274	**.09**	**E .002**	**.07**	< .007	< .04	< .020	< .02	**1.47**	**.27**	< .006
W1284	< .02	< .014	**.02**	< .007	< .04	< .020	< .02	**.07**	**.02**	< .006
WR1106	< .02	< .014	< .02	< .007	< .04	< .020	< .02	< .02	< .02	< .006
WR1280	< .02	< .014	< .02	< .007	< .08	< .016	< .04	< .02	< .02	< .006
WR1849	< .02	< .014	< .02	< .007	< .08	< .016	**M**	< .02	< .02	< .006

[1] EX, Essex County; FU, Fulton County; H, Hamilton County; RE, Rensselaer County; SA, Saratoga County; W, Washington County; WR, Warren County.

Table A7. Concentrations of volatile organic compounds and phenolic compounds detected in groundwater samples collected in the Upper Hudson River Basin, New York, 2007.

[μg/L, micrograms per liter; (32101), U.S. Geological Survey National Water Information System parameter code; <, less than. Bold values indicate detections. Well locations are shown in fig. 2.]

Well number[1]	Bromo-dichloro-methane, unfiltered, μg/L (32101)	Dibromo-chloro-methane, unfiltered, μg/L (32105)	Methyl *tert*-butyl ether, unfiltered, μg/L (78032)	Tetrachloro-ethene, unfiltered, μg/L (34475)	Toluene, unfiltered, μg/L (34010)	Trichloro-methane, unfiltered, μg/L (32106)	Total phenolic compounds, unfiltered, μg/L (32730)
Sand and gravel wells							
EX159	< 0.1	< 0.2	< 0.2	< 0.1	< 0.1	< 0.1	< 4
FU273	< .1	< .2	< .2	< .1	< .1	**.2**	< 4
H296	**.2**	< .2	< .2	< .1	< .1	**.5**	< 4
RE889	**.2**	< .2	< .2	< .1	< .1	**.4**	< 4
RE1768	< .1	< .2	< .2	< .1	< .1	**.1**	< 4
SA879	< .1	< .2	< .2	< .1	< .1	< .1	< 4
SA2742	< .1	< .2	**.3**	< .1	< .1	**.5**	< 4
SA3644	< .1	< .2	< .2	< .1	< .1	< .1	< 4
SA4024	< .1	< .2	**1.0**	< .1	< .1	< .1	< 4
SA4987	< .1	< .2	< .2	< .1	< .1	< .1	< 4
W1419	< .1	< .2	< .2	< .1	< .1	< .1	< 4
WR83	**.3**	**.2**	< .2	< .1	< .1	**.3**	< 4
WR85	< .1	< .2	< .2	**.3**	< .1	**1.0**	< 4
Bedrock wells							
EX797	< .1	< .2	< .2	< .1	< .1	< .1	< 4
EX1143	< .1	< .2	< .2	< .1	< .1	< .1	< 4
H56	< .1	< .2	**4.2**	< .1	< .1	**.2**	< 4
H401	< .1	< .2	< .2	< .1	< .1	< .1	< 4
H453	< .1	< .2	< .2	< .1	< .1	< .1	< 4
RE2694	< .1	< .2	< .2	< .1	< .1	< .1	< 4
SA4346	< .1	< .2	< .2	< .1	< .1	< .1	**5.1**
W1274	< .1	< .2	< .2	< .1	< .1	< .1	< 4
W1284	< .1	< .2	< .2	< .1	< .1	< .1	< 4
WR1106	< .1	< .2	< .2	< .1	< .1	< .1	< 4
WR1280	< .1	< .2	< .2	< .1	< .1	< .1	< 4
WR1849	< .1	< .2	< .2	< .1	**1.1**	< .1	< 4

[1] EX, Essex County; FU, Fulton County; H, Hamilton County; RE, Rensselaer County; SA, Saratoga County; W, Washington County; WR, Warren County.

Table A8. Bacteria in groundwater samples collected in the Upper Hudson River Basin, New York, 2007.

[CFU, colony-forming unit; mL, milliliter; (31691), U.S. Geological Survey National Water Information System parameter code; <, less than. Well locations are shown in fig. 2.]

Well number[1]	*Escherichia coli*, unfiltered, CFU/100mL (31691)	Fecal coliform, unfiltered, CFU/100mL (61215)	Heterotrophic plate count, unfiltered, CFU/mL (31692)	Total coliform, unfiltered, CFU/100mL (61213)
Sand and gravel wells				
EX159	< 1	< 1	1	< 1
FU273	< 1	< 1	5	< 1
H296	< 1	< 1	< 1	< 1
RE889	< 1	< 1	< 1	< 1
RE1768	< 1	< 1	< 1	< 1
SA879	< 1	< 1	< 1	< 1
SA2742	< 1	< 1	< 1	< 1
SA3644	< 1	< 1	< 1	< 1
SA4024	< 1	< 1	< 1	< 1
SA4987	< 1	< 1	52	< 1
W1419	< 1	< 1	< 1	< 1
WR83	< 1	< 1	< 1	< 1
WR85	< 1	< 1	< 1	< 1
Bedrock wells				
EX797	< 1	< 1	7	< 1
EX1143	< 1	< 1	< 1	< 1
H56	< 1	< 1	< 1	< 1
H401	< 1	< 1	47	24
H453	< 1	< 1	2	< 1
RE2694	< 1	< 1	16	< 1
SA4346	< 1	< 1	1	< 1
W1274	< 1	< 1	4	< 1
W1284	< 1	< 1	< 1	< 1
WR1106	< 1	< 1	< 1	< 1
WR1280	< 1	< 1	< 1	< 1
WR1849	< 1	< 1	252	< 1

[1] EX, Essex County; FU, Fulton County; H, Hamilton County; RE, Rensselaer County; SA, Saratoga County; W, Washington County; WR, Warren County.

This page has been left blank intentionally.

For more information concerning this report, contact

Director
U.S. Geological Survey
New York Water Science Center
425 Jordan Road
Troy, NY 12180-8349
dc_ny@usgs.gov

or visit our Web site at:
http://ny.water.usgs.gov

Nystrom—Groundwater Quality in the Upper Hudson River Basin, New York, 2007—Open-File Report 2009–1240